D1192262

HOW TO MAKE
A LIVING IN
ANTIQUES

HOW TO MAKE
A LIVING IN
ANTIQUES

WILLIAM C. KETCHUM, JR.

Henry Holt and Company

New York

Published by Henry Holt and Company, Inc.,
115 West 18th Street, New York, New York 10011.
Published in Canada by Fitzhenry & Whiteside Limited,
195 Allstate Parkway, Markham, Ontario L3R 4T8.

Library of Congress Cataloging-in-Publication Data
Ketchum, William C., 1931–
How to make a living in antiques / William C.
Ketchum, Jr.—1st ed.
p. cm.
Bibliography: p.
ISBN 0-8050-0998-1
1. Antiques—Marketing. 2. Antiques as an investment.
3. Selling—Antiques. I. Title.
NK1125.K48 1989
745.1'068—dc20 89-11214
CIP

Henry Holt books are available at special discounts
for bulk purchases for sales promotions, premiums,
fund-raising, or educational use. Special editions
or book excerpts can also be created to specification.
For details contact:
Special Sales Director
Henry Holt and Company, Inc.
115 West 18th Street
New York, New York 10011

First Edition

DESIGNED BY CLAIRE M. NAYLON
Printed in the United States of America
1   3   5   7   9   10   8   6   4   2

CONTENTS

INTRODUCTION

*A*lmost all of us love antiques and collectibles; for their beauty, for their power to evoke memories of the past, and for the warmth they give to the home. Small wonder then that, at a time when the number of small businesses in this country is increasing at an astonishing rate, more and more people are considering entering the antiques field.

The appeal is strong. We are all collectors at heart. What better way to earn a living than by doing what one enjoys? Moreover, anyone who reads the newspapers, listens to the radio, or watches television has heard of the phenomenal prices being paid for rare antiques and for much more recent collectibles, such as tickets to the Woodstock music festival or cookie jars once owned by Andy Warhol.

And much of what you hear is true. It is possible to make money in the antiques and collectibles business—lots of money—while having fun, learning, and meeting interesting new people. It is also possible, however, to fail. What this book is about is traveling the road to success while avoiding the pitfalls that dealers both neophyte and veteran may encounter.

The phenomenal growth of the antiques and collectibles

world over the past two decades has been due in part to a generalized prosperity and increase in leisure time, but it also reflects a widely held belief that it *is* possible, through buying, selling, and investing in antiques, to "get rich quick." Yet the reality can be something else. The pleasure may be there, but the profit often is not. In this highly competitive field, two out of three dealers go out of business within two years of start-up. Some were never heavily involved and simply retrench a bit, going back to collecting and whatever else they were doing for a living. For others, though, the experience is attended by bankruptcy, disruptions of their personal lives, and all the other indicia of a full-scale financial disaster.

The goal of this book is to help you, as a potential antiques and collectibles dealer, avoid this sort of misfortune by choosing the right business and running it in a way most likely to maximize profits and reduce losses.

It is important to understand first that antiques and collectibles are luxury items. No one really needs them. Consequently, the general market is very much dependent upon the nation's overall economic situation. When times are good and money is available, people will buy. A recession signals a sharp fall-off in purchases.

However, many dealers may not realize a recession is at hand, as most of the publicity surrounding the antiques and collectibles world is generated by the major auction houses, which sell to a tiny but very wealthy portion of the entire collecting community. These auction houses and the individuals and corporations who buy from them are seldom affected by business downturns and will continue to buy and sell for astronomical prices at times when middle-range dealers are going out of business and most collectors are having to spend their cash on necessities.

Thus, the first rule must be: Do not base your assessment

of the health of the antiques market on the prices being paid at Sotheby's and Christie's. Base it on the unemployment figures!

The field is also affected by two other important economic factors: the stock market and the value of the dollar in relation to foreign currencies. A sharp decline in the market, like the one in October 1987, may hurt sales by hurting the finances of potential buyers who are also stock owners. However, in a long-term decline, such as during the 1970s and early '80s, investors may decide to put their money into antiques and collectibles on the theory that they will obtain a greater return than what is currently promised by the stock market.

Regarding the relationship of the dollar to other national currencies, the early eighties were high times for many dealers who traded in imported antiques. With the dollar up, they could buy very favorably in Europe and sell at a large profit in this country. The dollar's decline in recent years has largely destroyed the import market (other than for cheap reproductions). On the other hand, prosperity in other countries has fueled the American antiques and collectibles boom. First, during the seventies, it was the oil-rich Near Eastern buyers purchasing Oriental rugs and a variety of other furnishings. Now, with their currencies riding high, the Japanese, West Germans, and other Common Market members are buying heavily.

If such factors seem pretty abstract to most beginning dealers, competition should provide a more concrete yardstick by which to measure potential success. There are tens of thousands of individuals, partnerships, and corporations engaged in the antiques and collectibles business. In 1988, New York State alone listed thirteen thousand! Anyone entering the field should be aware of this competition and be prepared to meet it through the sort of creative planning and aggressive merchandising described in this book.

However, other things, such as financial resources, being equal, knowledgeable dealers will succeed. They will do so because they know that the antiques and collectibles trade is a retail business (though with some unique qualities) requiring much the same business orientation as a shoe or appliance store. The customer, here as elsewhere, is the boss! Your job is to determine what appeals to him or her and to offer it at an affordable price. You will have to establish sources for your merchandise so that when you sell something it can be replaced by an item of comparable appeal. You will want to prove yourself trustworthy and knowledgeable so that your clients will come to rely on your honesty, taste, and judgment.

You should also be quick to adapt to the changes wrought in the field not only by economic considerations but also by matters of taste. The world of antiques and collectibles is by and large a faddish one. True, there are certain categories—fine furniture, silver, and old masters to name but a few—that have held their value for generations. But many items suddenly rise to popularity only to decline within a few years. The sharp dealer catches the crest of the wave and is out of the field when the collapse comes. The less fortunate are always just far enough behind a trend to buy when things are most expensive and to be holding a large inventory when interest has faded. Be a trendsetter, not a follower.

There are ways you can forecast changes in collecting habits. For example, museum exhibits or major books may draw attention to a hitherto unexplored field. These will be followed by auctions at which the items from that field suddenly begin to bring much higher prices than previously realized. If the collectibles in question are available in sufficient quantity, collectors' clubs will appear. Within a short time the new field will be the subject of newspaper and magazine articles, and well-known movie and television personalities will be photographed in their homes surrounded by these suddenly desirable pieces.

However, this is no guarantee of long-term stability in the market. Several factors can bring down a fad as quickly as it rose. Perhaps the worst are reproductions and fakes. Once it is known that these exist in quantity, interest quickly declines. In recent years, we saw this decline in the areas of pressed glass and scrimshaw.

Abundance can be another headache. Factory-made accessories and furniture of the 1950s were wildly popular in some circles until it became evident that individual items exist by the tens of thousands. With this realization, most up-scale collectors left the field. Many dealers are still earning a living in the fifties field, but they are mostly catering to a broad public of middle-range enthusiasts who expect to pay modest prices for relatively common objects.

There also seem to be little-understood cycles in public taste. Hooked rugs, for example, were popular in the 1920s, then disappeared from public view until the early 1970s, sank again, and have now been rediscovered. The astute dealer will chart these ups and downs of the market by subscribing to trade papers, antiques and collectibles magazines, auction catalogs, and museum bulletins and will always try to be just a little ahead of a developing trend.

You should also recognize that the role of the antiques and collectibles dealer has changed greatly in the past few decades and continues to change. Once the dealer was an antiquarian steeped in knowledge of a narrow field or was little more than an eccentric junk dealer. Today's dealer must be part investment counselor, part interior decorator, and part art critic, always ready to explain, defend, and justify his or her merchandise in the constantly changing world of public taste. Those who enjoy this sort of challenge and are quick to adapt to changes and to exploit new markets will do well.

In the following chapters we will talk about the various facets of the dealer's craft, from the best ways in which to buy, advertise, display, and sell antiques and collectibles to such mundane but important matters as shop security, bookkeeping, and storage. As in any area of life, there is no guarantee of success, but anyone who reads this book and takes its lessons to heart should be well able to realize this most coveted and rewarding career.

HOW TO MAKE
A LIVING IN
ANTIQUES

1.

CHOOSING A FIELD

In the antiques and collectibles world, dealers often don't choose their areas of specialization; the areas choose them. Unlike most retail businesses, where one may simply buy a franchise or go into an available field because it looks profitable, almost all antiques dealers are drawn to the profession by a prior interest. Most are collectors who started out selling simply to upgrade their own collections and gradually found that the life—the wheeling and dealing and the possibility of profit—got the better of them.

Certainly, in one sense this is a far better way to get started. You may find dealers disgruntled about their profits, about the auction houses, about their competition; but you will find few who complain about what they do. However, in order for this fun to be profitable as well, you have to make a realistic choice as to a field of specialization.

Defining your area of the antiques and collectibles world involves defining yourself. If you are the gregarious type, you will probably like "show business," that is, running a large general shop in an area where you will have lots of walk-in trade. On the other hand, a studious individual fascinated by details of history and technology will probably not enjoy constant contact with people who neither understand nor appreciate his or her field of interest. For him, or for her, the answer may be specialization, with either a small, out-of-the-way shop or no shop at all—relying instead on mail order or shows with a sharp focus on things such as weapons, Arts and Crafts, or Orientalia.

The majority of dealers, though, strike a balance where the business emphasizes the owner's strongest areas in terms of knowledge and preference but also reflects more general tastes. It is usually difficult, particularly for beginning dealers, to specialize in a single area, because it requires a substantial specialized clientele, something it takes years to build up. In the meantime, you will want to have something for the many other potential clients with whom you may come into contact. Moreover, the most successful dealers are usually those who combine a broad, general knowledge with their area of specialization. If you take this approach, when presented with a house full of antiques or an offer of some items from a "drop-in" seller, you'll be able to pick those things on which you can make money even though these may not be what you are really interested in.

The dealer in Battersea boxes, netsuke, and similar small but precious items, who can spot and evaluate an eighteenth-century Dutch armoire or a rare early French touring car, is a person who can continually supplement his or her regular income with great finds.

Knowledge and interest are two factors that will dictate your choice of field, but there are other practical considerations as well. Finances are a major concern. Opening and operating a shop usually involves a considerable financial expenditure. Being a show or mail-order dealer may be a necessity, at least early in your career. On the other hand, an active show schedule is physically demanding—too much so for many older dealers.

In every instance the best rule is to start small. Don't bite off too much in the first months or years, either in terms of financial outlay or commitment of time and physical energy. Many dealers sour on the field just because they expect too much too fast. They may have also chosen the wrong location or the wrong business for that location. While, over a period of time, a knowledgeable, persuasive dealer can have substantial effect on the taste and preferences of his or her customers, you cannot hope to come into a community with something that does not interest buyers and expect them to change their buying habits overnight.

If you are an authority on art glass or pre-Christian antiquities and wish to run an open shop, you had best locate in a large city with a substantial number of sophisticated local buyers. On the other hand, there are many wonderful antiques and collectibles that will appeal to buyers in smaller communities. Depression glass and Fiesta-ware pottery from the 1930s are popular in many parts of the South and Midwest. Dealers in old guns and antique fishing tackle may also find a bonanza in such areas.

But be sure that your price levels fit within the parameters of the local economy. A depressed industrial town is not the best place to establish a business in fine jewelry or costly fabrics. You might, however, do quite well with moderately priced items—kitchen collectibles like tin, woodenware, and baskets, or the still-inexpensive furniture from the 1900 to 1940 era. If you give your customers attractive, useful collectibles at prices they can afford, you should do well anywhere.

There is another, more subtle consideration. Can you really bring yourself to sell what you love? In most retail areas this would be an absurd question. Can we really imagine a seller of farm equipment or prefabricated houses being unable to part with his or her wares? Of course not! Yet there are antiques and collectibles dealers who fail because they cannot really bear to part with the best things they acquire. They want to sell the junk and keep the treasure. Yet it is the treasure that builds your reputation. Every major dealer in every field has developed an impersonal attitude toward his or her stock and so must you. Otherwise, remain a collector!

2.

FINANCING

A lack of capital is the chief reason that antiques and collectibles businesses fail. No matter how knowledgeable you are, how many sources of merchandise you have, and what sort of rapport you may have established with your clients, if you do not have enough money both to pay your running expenses and replenish your stock, you will probably go under.

Since each individual business situation differs, it is really not possible to provide a specific guide on avoiding financial woes. However, certain pitfalls are easy to define and, with a small amount of consideration, easy to avoid. One of the most common errors beginners—especially those opening shops—tend to make is to overestimate income. The assumption is that one can rent a store, stock it, and then go into business with financial reserves amounting to no more than two or three months' overhead costs, and that overhead beyond that time will be covered by sales.

However, competition in this field is too tough for a novice dealer reasonably to believe that he or she can generate sufficient income in the first year or so of business to both cover overhead and buy new inventory. What usually happens is that profits go into rent, electricity, and the like, while stock on hand steadily declines, and the dealer is unable to replenish due to lack of funds. Without new items to draw in customers, the business tapers off—often to the point of closure.

Those knowledgeable in the retail business in general recommend that you not open your doors without sufficient savings or other guaranteed resources to cover at least one year's overhead. This way, whatever money the business earns can be ploughed back into it in the form of new stock.

But, you may ask, what do I live on? This brings us to the second pitfall and the second general rule: When entering into the new endeavor, avoid giving up established sources of income, or, "Don't quit your day job!" While the antiques and collectibles field is often the very best retail answer for the individual with retirement income or some other steady source of funds, it is seldom the right move for someone who depends solely on a weekly or monthly salary.

If, on the other hand, you can't wait until retirement to get your feet wet, the answer may be selling at antiques shows or operating from your home. You can run a part-time, low-overhead business while still maintaining your other career. If you must have a store, operate it on weekends only, since that is when the vast majority of your business will be transacted; or employ someone to staff it during the work week.

Another trap to watch out for is trying to take on too much too soon. The tendency of some novice dealers, especially if they have been successful initially, is to try to move immediately into the big time—expanding shop size, doing the major shows, advertising in the glossy magazines, and so forth.

Remember that most of the top dealers "paid their dues"; that is, they spent years building a clientele, establishing sources for better-quality merchandise, and nurturing a reputation that would assure them entry into the major shows. You cannot duplicate this overnight. Certainly an abundance of money can create a façade of respectability that will, perhaps, fool some of the nouveau riche. However, most well-to-do collectors are unimpressed with such tactics. They buy from long-established dealers, and your time and money will be better spent buying quality merchandise and establishing a reputation for knowledge and integrity.

Besides, if you are like most newly minted dealers, you do not have money to throw around. Therefore, you should

1. Take a shop space that you can afford; usually, your rent should not exceed ten percent of your gross annual sales.

2. Avoid costly advertising campaigns; an advertising budget of around two to three percent of gross annual sales is about right.

3. Keep fixed expenses such as utilities and telephone low by economizing on light and heat (lights, for example, may be kept low in many areas of a shop when customers are not present) and by not using the telephone to while away your boring hours. Dealers are notorious chatterboxes. Confine your outgoing calls to ones that will really generate business.

Obtaining Money for the Business

No matter how *wisely* you spend, you must have something to spend. Obtaining seed money for any retail business can be a frustrating endeavor. However, recent media attention directed at the profits to be realized in the antiques and collectibles field has made it somewhat less difficult.

Exactly how eager banks, other lending institutions, and private parties will be to finance your business will usually depend on two factors: your overall credit/financial situation and your business experience.

The best place to start is your own bank. Have a talk with a financial officer, outlining your business prospects. Include a projection of expenses (such as rent, utilities, telephone, advertising, insurance, and various federal and state taxes), profits, and any outside income, which can be worked up with the aid of an accountant. The bank may be interested in loaning you money, or, at the least, should be able to steer you to other possible sources of funds. Needless to say, if you are planning (against my advice!) to abandon full-time employment for the world of antiques and collectibles, your visit to the bank should be made before you leave your job.

The more assets you have, the more likely it is that you will be able to obtain an initial loan. Few lenders are interested in unsecured advances. A first or second mortgage on your home or other real estate is one form of creditor protection. Chattel mortgages covering everything from automobiles to inventory may secure promissory notes. The risks, however, are obvious. If the business goes sour, you may also lose everything else. Be very cautious!

Other possible sources of capital include small-business loans obtained from agencies of the state or federal government, loans from credit unions, and, on a very short-term basis, cash advances on your credit cards. In all cases, however, need for the funds should be weighed against both the interest to be paid for use of the money and the risks of default. When in doubt, see your accountant.

Today, increasingly, an important source of capital is the individual investor. Impressed by tales, generated by the auction houses, of the fabulous profits to be made in the antiques world, more and more wealthy investors are backing antiques dealers as an alternative to putting their funds into more traditional areas, such as real estate or the stock market.

The investor may either make loans to the business, usually secured by short-term promissory notes, or may actually acquire a stake in it as a silent partner or, when you have incorporated, as a stockholder. Many dealers prefer the latter options, in which the investor then has a long-term interest in the business, an interest in its future, instead of being just a creditor. On the other hand, such investments may dilute the control you have over your own business. Again, it's a good idea to talk to your lawyer or accountant before entering into such an arrangement.

Whatever your source of financial backing, you should strive to maintain a low ratio of debt to assets, so that if you are suddenly forced to pay off your loans you can do so without destroying your business. No matter how tempting the ideas of expansion, upgrading merchandise, or image manipulation may be, they should never be undertaken at the risk of falling uncontrollably into debt.

3.
LEGAL AND ACCOUNTING
CONSIDERATIONS

*W*hen in doubt see a lawyer or an accountant! Without question, this is the best advice that anyone entering into a small-business venture can ever be given. Yet far too many antiques and collectibles dealers blunder into and sometimes through their careers without recourse to legal and financial advice, or seek assistance only after they have encountered a serious problem.

There are many laws that will have an impact on your business, including those having to do with zoning, building codes, health and sanitation, rubbish removal, historic preservation (which may affect what you can do to the outside of your building or even what sort of signs you can install), and safety regulations. These vary from state to state and even from locality to locality. Moreover, federal, state, and local tax laws change yearly. No one untrained in these fields can hope to keep current, and it is essential that you have a professional to turn to, not only at tax time, but whenever a question arises that may affect your business.

Neither this nor any other single book can provide the information necessary to protect you from legal and tax problems. However, it is possible to lay down some general guidelines that will indicate certain occasions on which you should seek technical guidance.

Choosing a Business Structure

Most antiques dealers run their businesses either alone or in partnership with one or more fellow enthusiasts, but few bother to consider the consequences of these choices or to discuss the alternatives with a lawyer. The very beginning of your career may be when legal advice is most important. No one should go into business without sitting down first with his or her attorney.

Often, the first question on the table is that of business structure. There are only three basic structures: you can run your business alone, as a partnership, or as a corporation. The choice you make will subject you to different legal and tax consequences, and your adviser will explain these to you in detail, setting forth the advantages and disadvantages of each in regard to your locality and your individual financial situation.

The following general information is offered only to provide a framework for understanding legal and accounting advice and should not be regarded as a recommendation for any particular course of action. Only your attorney or accountant can provide that.

Most antiques and collectibles dealers operate alone, as individual proprietors. They buy and sell on their own account and file a Schedule C with their federal tax return setting forth their profit or loss for the year. An individual proprietorship gives you both the greatest freedom and the greatest responsibility. All the profits are yours, but so are the losses; and if the business fails, leaving outstanding debts, you can anticipate that creditors will in most cases have the right to seek payment out of personal assets, such as your home or automobile, that were not even involved in the business.

Partnerships have several advantages. They mean more bodies in the business, someone to do shows with or to watch the shop while you are out buying. They may also mean an infusion of cash into an undercapitalized business. The classic example of the latter is the so-called "silent partner," who advances money against a written agreement for repayment and a certain percentage of the profits but who takes no part in active management. More typical are active partners who are fully engaged in the business. The duties and limitations of each partner can be clearly defined in the articles of partnership. In most cases, all of the partners involved are equals who can buy and sell as freely as if they were individual proprietors. The major pitfalls of such an arrangement usually arise out of that buying and selling.

Your partner, in the eyes of the law and those you do business with, is you. Your partner can buy, and the seller can look to you for payment even if you did not approve, or were not even aware of, the transaction. Taxes due from the partnership may be levied upon and collected from either or both partners. An absconding partner can leave you with a pile of debts while running off with the chief assets of the firm. Of course, you can sue him (if you can find him!), but obviously your goal is always to avoid getting to that point.

That's where the lawyer comes in. A carefully drafted partnership agreement should protect all parties as far as is possible under applicable law, defining obligations, limiting the powers to buy and sell where necessary (for example, positing that purchases above a certain sum must be approved by more than one member), and generally defining the ground rules of the relationship. The time to seek such partnership advice is before you and your friend or neighbor start buying and selling together. In most cases, once you hold yourselves out to the public as partners, those with whom you do business may treat you as such, with all the attendant legal consequences.

The third structure, the corporation, is generally designed

to limit individual liability and to provide tax advantages where available. In broad terms, those who invest in a corporate venture (that is, buy stock) are responsible for the corporation's debts only to the extent of their investment. Given the broad scope of liability for debts or taxes that exists in individual proprietorships and partnerships, the corporation might seem to have immediate appeal for many. However, advice of counsel may convince them otherwise.

Where any sizable sum is involved, most people or institutions who sell or lend to a small corporation will require the personal guarantee of an officer (usually the same person who is trying to avoid personal liability!). Moreover, although a few short years ago federal tax laws favored small corporations with lower rates and encouraged this arrangement even for small businesses, such as antiques shops, the law presently provides no such advantages. Finally—though this may be a relatively small consideration in light of the greater business picture—it is no small expense to have an attorney prepare articles of incorporation, do a corporate-name search, and purchase a corporate "kit" (minute book, seal, etc.).

Even this brief outline should make it clear that your choice of business structure is a serious decision, and one that should be determined only after consultation with a qualified adviser.

Among other matters your attorney will discuss with you are sales taxes and resale numbers. Many, though by no means all, states impose a sales tax on many purchases (medicines, most foods, and some other necessities are customarily excluded). Antiques dealers, like other merchants, are required to collect this tax for the state and to remit it on a quarterly or semiannual basis.

Dealers are also required to purchase a resale number that serves as a form of identification for their business with state and local taxing authorities. The benefit to you of the resale number is that it allows you to buy merchandise without paying sales tax; you are purchasing for "resale," not as the ultimate consumer, and it is the consumer upon whom, in theory, the tax is laid. Since sales taxes can be substantial (in some jurisdictions they may run as high as ten percent), the possession of a sales-tax number can be deemed so desirable that even some nondealer collectors put up with the inconvenience of filing business tax returns in order to avoid paying it—and, incidentally, to obtain the further advantage of the "dealer's" discount, which is nearly automatic with a resale number.

Bookkeeping

Once you are in business you should normally have recourse to an attorney only when confronted with a major decision such as the purchase or rental of space (every store lease should be reviewed by your lawyer), conflicts with partners or third parties, accidents that raise the possibility of your being sued or suing others, or tax liability questions. Your accountant may be more often on the scene, counseling you regarding preparation of annual tax returns and the myriad complexities involved if you have employees (social security, withholding taxes, et cetera).

Constantly with you, though, will be the problems of bookkeeping. You must either employ a bookkeeper (full-time or part-time) or learn to keep adequate records yourself. Everyone in the antiques and collectibles business has a story about the dealer in business thirty years who keeps everything in his or her head, never worries about collecting sales taxes, and always makes money.

I knew one of these people. A few years ago she came to open her shop one morning and found a big padlock (not her own!) on the door along with a Notice of Seizure. The state was planning to sell the contents of her shop to satisfy its sales-tax claims. She was understandably upset, but she also still be-

lieved in another old myth, that you can drive the tax authorities crazy by presenting them with the "shoe box" full of sales
receipts and then letting them try to figure out the tax liability.

So she handed the auditor the shoe box. He didn't turn a
hair; he simply levied against her bank accounts for what he
calculated the taxes due might be and gave her back the box.
She had to reconstruct three years of sales in order to get back
in action!

Now that you are treating the buying and selling of antiques
and collectibles as a business, you must function as a busi-
nessperson, and that means good record keeping. At a minimum, a good bookkeeping system should provide you with
more or less instant access to two types of information: the
individual history from purchase to sale of each item that passes
through your hands, and all expenditures that may be taken as
tax deductions against business income.

The first is a relatively simple matter of record keeping. You
can quickly set up a running or "perpetual" inventory system
using a lined looseleaf notebook. In this you should record each
purchase under the following headings: *date of purchase, stock
number, description, from whom purchased, cost, your
method of payment, selling price, buyer's method of payment.*

The stock numbers can start at any point, but a three-digit
system—001, 002—is usually preferable. Use of stock numbers
on your price tags provides you or your employees with instant
reference to the history of a given object in stock, while a
description of the item (including whatever of its history you
might have been able to learn) may provide the kind of provenance a buyer is looking for.

Much of this information, such as the names of sellers and
method of payment, could, of course, be reconstructed from
other sources, like canceled checks or receipts; but having it all
quickly at hand is far more helpful. Moreover, by reference to
your inventory you can at any time determine the net or
purchase value of your current stock, and at the end of the year

you can also quickly learn your gross profit and net merchandise cost. The latter, incidentally, should include any repair expense attributable to a particular purchase.

Another important element of record keeping is the preparation of an invoice covering each business transaction, whether a purchase or sale. For purchases you should insist on a receipt that includes date, amount, description of merchandise (discussed in chapter 6, "Buying from Other Dealers"), and the seller's name. Your own invoices should include price, method of payment, stock number, date, name of purchaser and his or her resale number (if applicable), as well as discount, if any. Normally, two copies of a receipt (one for buyer, one for seller) are sufficient, but if you sell things on layaway you may want a third, which can be filed separately and used to keep track of payments until the piece eventually passes to the customer.

Keeping track of costs is another, equally important, matter. Before you go into business you should sit down with your accountant or tax attorney and get his or her advice as to both what is legally tax deductible and what documentation is necessary to support those deductions. In general, everything properly connected to the furtherance of your business is potentially deductible. Obviously, all purchases, restorations to make items suitable for resale, booth rentals, and shop costs, such as rent, light, heat, and business telephone calls should fall within this broad category.

However, many other costs, which you might not think of, may be deductible. Meals, motel rooms, and car expenses connected with the doing of a show or a legitimate buying trip should be carefully documented with canceled checks or cash receipts. Not surprisingly, the IRS looks closely at these less intrinsic expenses. Winter buying trips to Florida, especially if your party includes the whole family and the shops you deal with seem all to be located in coastal resorts, will raise a red flag.

If the expense is legitimate, don't hesitate to deduct it. Just be sure to collect the proper documentation along the way.

Likewise, it may be possible to deduct tuition, room and board, and other costs directly related to your attendance at a seminar designed to improve your ability to run your business, or the purchase of books in the field acquired for your research library.

There is more than this to record keeping, as a good book-keeper will quickly show you, but if you maintain at least these minimal records you should be able to both preserve your attorney or accountant's sanity and protect yourself from the onslaughts of tax officials. You might even have an idea of what you are earning!

Insurance

Anyone doing shows or running a shop needs to be concerned about two forms of insurance: liability coverage and fire-and-theft. Again, as with legal and accounting questions, have recourse to a knowledgeable professional, in this case your insurance broker.

Liability insurance protects you against claims by people who might be injured while in your shop or show booth (the classic "slip on the banana peel" case). This coverage is absolutely essential, whatever the cost, and is usually required to rent space at an antiques mall or shopping center, where the management also customarily requires that it be included under your policy protection.

Fire, theft, and sundry loss insurance covers damages you incur either through the acts of individuals (vandalism or robbery, for example) or acts of God, such as fires, earthquakes, and floods. Sad to say, theft rates in many areas of the country

(New York City, Los Angeles, Detroit, and Washington, D.C., for example) are so high as to be prohibitive for most new dealers.

Many dealers who carry relatively less valuable items become what is euphemistically termed "self-insurers," that is, they have no insurance. Another alternative is to choose a policy with a very high deductible, say a thousand dollars, so that your rates are lower and you are at least protected from the heaviest losses.

If you do decide to carry insurance, you will have the satisfaction of knowing that it is (at the moment) tax deductible.

At a time when everyone from doctors to architects is complaining about high insurance rates, it may be very tempting just to forget about the whole thing. That is something no dealer can afford to do. Fire-and-theft insurance is one thing, since the burden of loss extends only to those objects destroyed or stolen. Liability insurance is another matter. If you fail to insure against accidents to those entering your shop, home, or booth, you run the risk of exposing yourself and your family to a catastrophic court judgment. Insurance is a reasonable business expense. Be sure you have it.

Finally, let me remind you again that such considerations as legal and accounting problems and insurance coverage, while certainly far less interesting than the buying and selling of antiques and collectibles, are the key to running a professional (and successful) business. Ignore them at your peril!

4·

BUYING

That old retail axiom, "You can't sell without buying," is nowhere more appropriate than in the antiques field. Moreover, one will find few dealers who prefer selling to buying: for most, sales are just a necessity, something they have to do in order to have money to buy. It is the love of the chase and the acquisition of the rare and the beautiful that turn them on.

In fact, it is really the problems and challenges of buying that separate this field from other retail businesses. Since antiques and quality collectibles are, if not one-of-a-kind objects, available only in limited numbers, the replenishment of stock is always an issue.

When the shoe salesman has a run on a popular tennis shoe, he or she just calls up the local distributor and orders another dozen pairs. Increase in demand for everything from clothing to household appliances and popular magazines can quickly be met through calls to manufacturers and their agents. The antiques dealer, on the other hand, is in a unique position. Even mass-produced items, such as tin toys of the 1930s or Fiesta ware of the same vintage, are not any longer instantly available. When an item is sold, its replacement may involve anything from a few calls to other dealers or collectors to a national or international pursuit involving numerous inquiries, long hours on the road, and, in most instances, the payment of a higher price than was paid for the original piece.

As most newly minted antiques dealers are also collectors, in many cases of long standing, they tend to enter the field with a substantial inventory. Usually, this has been acquired over a considerable period of time and in a rather leisurely manner. There has been no particular compulsion to buy (other than the natural lust for acquisition, of course), and, if the collector is knowledgeable, condition and price have been prime considerations.

As a dealer, you are faced with a very different situation. Satisfying the customer is a paramount consideration. If a collector or another dealer wants a certain item and wants it *now* (as is usually the case), there is no time for dallying. It's on the road and on the quest.

But, of course, merely finding the desired antique is not the end of it. The piece must be in a condition to satisfy not only the dealer but also the potential customer; and it must be priced for resale. That is, you can only pay a price that will allow for a markup that gives you a reasonable profit and at the same time is sufficiently competitive to prevent the potential customer from looking elsewhere.

This is a dilemma you will face frequently as a neophyte dealer. You must replenish your wares at prices substantially above those you paid several years ago for similar merchandise.

Understanding Prices

However, there is an even more universal problem, which all antiques and collectibles dealers must address each time they buy. That is the question of valuation. In order to *buy* successfully, you must know the approximate retail *selling* price of those goods you wish to sell. Again, this is not a great problem in most retail fields, where prices are both fairly stabilized and well-known in the trade. But there is no such certainty in the antiques world. Many variables affect the figure at which a specific item may be sold: its rarity, desirability, condition, the knowledge of buyer and seller, dealer reputation, the region in which a piece is offered, and even the time of year (wicker, for example, brings higher prices in spring than in winter!).

It is not an easy matter to gain a broad working knowledge of antiques and collectibles prices within your area of interest. Indeed, many dealers never do, and thus many great buys slip through their hands into the grasp of the more astute.

For the beginner or for the less ambitious, price guides are the first recourse. These slickly packaged paperbacks offer price estimates either on a broad general field of antiques and collectibles or on a specific area, such as bottles or dolls. Since the former, though they may boast of "thousands of prices," can never hope to cover everything in the field, they are inherently incomplete (and somehow it is always the item you have or want that is left out!). The more focused guides are more helpful.

However, in all cases, price guides have certain fundamental limitations. Few are well illustrated, leaving the collector to puzzle out whether or not such a description as "blue decorated crock with flower . . . $125" really applies in any meaningful way to the piece of stoneware he or she just acquired. Prices are taken from a variety of sources, in most cases throughout the country, but do not really deal with the problem of regional pricing differentials. Condition, so vital in pricing (a chip or crack may devalue a piece of old glass as much as eighty percent), is usually ignored or avoided by a general statement such as "damaged pieces are less valuable" or "discount up to fifty percent for serious damage." Moreover, in a thin market where a relatively few buyers are competing for the top items— a situation that now exists, for example, in the Arts and Crafts field—there simply may not be enough transactions to base price guidelines on. Finally, guides quickly become outdated in a rapidly rising market.

Taking all this into account, price guides such as the ubiquitous *Kovels'* and *Warman's* do have a function in pricing. When properly used by an informed dealer (for all guides assume certain general knowledge about the fields covered), they do provide broad guidelines that may be particularly helpful when trying to determine whether or not to make a purchase.

Another much-touted source of pricing information is the auction market. Capitalizing on the public's curiosity about auction results, Sotheby's and Christie's, the two major American auction houses, have taken to producing their own price guides based on their yearly auction tabulations. They and many large regional auction houses also sell catalogs covering their auctions, and these are priced following the event.

Of course, neither the objects sold nor the prices realized at these high-end auction houses have any real meaning for the vast majority of American antiques and collectibles dealers. How could they, when the "big two" will not usually even accept lots valued at less than a thousand dollars? Most dealers seldom handle things approaching that minimum. On the other hand, local auction results can be extremely helpful in establishing regional prices for more ordinary goods, such as toys and dolls, oak furniture, and common glass and pottery—things that exist in such quantity and appear frequently enough on the block that a "standard" price may be generated.

Frequency of appearance is the key to auction valuation. Items that rarely surface in the market but are avidly sought after will often skew the results, as you can readily see by comparing the estimates and the prices realized at the major houses. There it is not uncommon for a rarity to bring three or four times its estimate.

At the other end of the spectrum, low-end items, which may sell in the five-to-ten-dollar range for many dealers, will often be combined at auction into box lots selling for a dollar or so. On the basis of the auction results, these pieces would seem to have little or no value. Not so. While it is not profitable for an auctioneer to sell these pieces one at a time for a dollar or two each, a dealer can do so and make double the cost of a box lot.

Other things that may lead to abnormal auction results are failure of the auctioneer to recognize and promote the rarity and value of an item, unpredictable factors such as weather and competing events that may decrease attendance among the active bidders, the presence of bidding rings that depress prices, and "auction fever," which may drive bidders to pay far more than they should just to attract attention or "show up" a competitor.

Finally, we should mention the celebrity factor. Even the most ordinary items, if owned by a person in the public eye, may bring figures far in excess of their true market value. But that doesn't carry over to the general market. There is little lasting effect on the market, as was dramatically illustrated by the recent auction of the Andy Warhol collection. Among the thousands of things the artist had accumulated were dozens of factory-made figural cookie jars. Both auctioneer and public were astounded when these brought prices ranging into the thousands of dollars. However, no one was greatly astounded when dealers who subsequently raised the prices on identical jars found they had no takers. With items of little intrinsic worth, what counts is who owned them.

In short, auction results can be helpful in arriving at the value of an antique or collectible, but they should always be read against the background of the event itself—whose estate it was, who was there, what they knew, where it was held, and the like.

A more helpful guide, for the most part, are the prices charged by experienced dealers. People who have been in the trade for a few years usually see enough merchandise to develop a certain feel for prices, and again, except for the rare or greatly sought after items, prices assume a certain uniformity among these dealers.

This is particularly evidenced at antiques shows. When the dealers are setting up before the show opens, it often happens that several have an identical item, for example, an Imari bowl. Sometimes the prices asked will be quite close, within ten dollars of each other (differences that can, perhaps, be accounted for by condition or color). Sometimes there will be a great variance. One dealer will offer the bowl for $65. Another will want $130 for what is essentially the same piece. Before the opening, one of two things will happen. Either the lower-priced piece, if greatly undervalued, will be purchased for stock by a more knowledgeable dealer or competitive factors will cause the prices to telescope. The $65 bowl will be repriced at $95, while the more expensive one will be reduced to $115.

One of the best ways to obtain a broad general education in market values is by attending lots of antiques shows, especially the middle-range ones where neither the assumed prestige of the dealers nor the high costs of booth rentals force prices toward the upper limits.

Visiting shops can also be helpful. While an antiques-shop owner does not have quite the same public pressure toward uniformity that a show dealer has, he or she is certainly aware of what the competition is charging and usually will find it necessary to meet those prices. This is especially evident in a group shop, where the pressures that influence pricing decisions are the same as those of antiques shows.

Another good source of pricing information is the long-time collector. A knowledgeable enthusiast is acutely aware of the price structure in his or her field—often more so, in fact, than the general dealer or the auctioneer. Having a few collector friends can be a great help in pricing those tough exotics.

As you will by now have judged, pricing is really an art. It is not a skill you can acquire from reading a book. It requires active study and involvement with all elements of the antiques and collectibles world from auctions to shows, shops, and collectors.

Sources

Knowing what to pay and to charge is of little value if you cannot find merchandise to sell. With the phenomenal increase in the number of antiques and collectibles dealers and the competition for better items posed by the auction houses, it has become progressively more difficult for the individual dealer to obtain stock sufficient to provide customers with appealing choices. Some have attempted to resolve this problem by selling reproductions, crafts, or gift items, but by so doing they have in many cases removed themselves from the category of the true antiques dealer. For such merchants there is a flourishing world of reproductions extending from Taiwan to Trinidad.

However, for the dealer who wishes to sell only period items (be the period 1750 or 1950), there is no such easy solution. One cannot simply call up a supplier or "craftsman." It is necessary to seek out actively the sources of fresh merchandise, through auction, other dealers, private parties, or charitable organizations. This involves work, but the good news is that the "merch" is there. It has not all been gobbled up by auction houses or wealthy collectors. Finding it, though, can take some doing.

"To go or stay, that is the question." For decades, many antiques dealers were able to sit in their shops confident in the knowledge that picker-dealers or just ordinary folk with a yen for pocket money and surplus furnishings would bring goodies to the door. This still happens, but an increasing general knowledge of antiques' values and the ever-present auctioneer with his or her seemingly endless supply of money have put a crimp in the system. More and more local suppliers insist on valuing their possessions at retail prices or turn to the auction rooms. As a consequence, the dealer is forced more than ever to seek out new sources and to guard those sources.

Confidentiality is a relative matter, though, and even if you hide behind posts in the auction hall and use buying agents, it is often difficult to keep others from knowing that you are purchasing at auction. On the other hand, if you buy well from a country (or city) dealer or from private parties, you should keep that to yourself. There are other ways to show your generosity!

5.

BUYING AT AUCTION

*F*ew antiques dealers have kind words for the auction industry, and there is little doubt that the competition of cash-rich auction galleries has seriously affected the ability of dealers to buy from private parties and estates. On the other hand, the publicity generated by these same galleries has been the major factor in the spread of antiques fever throughout the United States, thus indirectly improving the business climate for antiques and collectibles dealers.

Moreover, most people in the antiques business buy at auction, and "the trade," as it is known, provides an important part of the income for every auction house from New York City to San Francisco. You, too, can and probably should buy at auction, and by learning a few simple rules you can do so profitably.

Auction-House Structure

It is important, as a potential buyer, that you know something about the nature of the auction business. In concept it is very simple. The auctioneer, acting either on his (or her) own behalf (as owner of the goods) or as agent for a third party (the consignor) offers a "lot" (which may consist of one or more objects) to the assembled public. Various members of the audience bid on it, the final, highest offer gaining the prize.

Upon this basic framework has been built a nationwide auction system consisting essentially of three levels. At the top are the two large international auction houses, Sotheby's and Christie's in New York City, which dominate the high end of the business and through their clever publicity staffs and social connections (Blue Book registry rather than antiques background is often the key to initial employment here) create an image of high prices and rare finds that permeates the entire market.

Just below, in an expanding pyramid, are the important regional auction houses, many of which gross millions of dollars each year and which may, on occasion, take estates away from the giants. Names such as Garth's of Ohio, Morton's of New Orleans, Skinner and Bourne of Massachusetts, Doyle's of New York, and Weschler's of Washington, D.C., are well-known to the trade.

Finally, there is the vast underpinning of the entire system—the thousands of local galleries scattered throughout the country. Some are well-known, highly successful, and the producers of dozens of auction events each year; others struggle along on dealers' castoffs and household cleanouts, selling everything from pots and pans to the rare, honest antique.

Auction Procedures

There is much more to the auction game than the simple selling system outlined above, and successful bidders make it a point to understand how each auction house operates. In the first place, the auctioneer earns his money in two ways: from the commission he charges those who consign items to him and, increasingly, from the buyer's premium extracted from winning bidders.

Commission is calculated as a percentage of the gross price at which a lot sells. If, for example, a table brings $300, and the commission agreed upon with its owner is 20 percent, the auctioneer earns $60. Typically, the auction commission is 10 to 15 percent, but it may vary greatly. Specialty galleries, such as those selling dolls and toys, may charge up to 33 percent, while a major auction house seeking to wrest an important estate away from a competitor may settle for 5 percent or even less.

In the latter instance, the auctioneer will make his money through the second half of our equation, the buyer's premium. Introduced from England nearly two decades ago, the premium, despite initial howls of rage from buyers, has become part of our system. It works just like the commission, but is applied at the other end of the transaction. If you were the buyer of the $300 table and the premium was, as it usually is, 10 percent, you would pay the house $300 plus $30. The latter sum goes to the gallery. The consignor would not share in it.

Though viewed by some as just another example of auction-gallery greed, the premium was introduced primarily to increase consignments. With it, the auctioneer could charge consignors a commission of as little as 5 to 10 percent and still make money. What this means to you, as a bidder, is that when deciding what you will pay for a lot you must factor in the buyer's premium. Is the table still a good buy at $330 rather than $300?

Another important element in the auction process is the reserve—that is, the price agreed upon between consignor and auctioneer, below which a piece will not be sold. Let us say that our table had had a reserve of $200. If the bidding had stopped at $180, the piece would have been "bought back," as they say in the trade. In such cases there may also be a penalty or "buy-in" fee of 3 to 5 percent of the reserve, which the consignor pays the gallery to cover, in part, the auctioneer's costs.

There is, of course, some inconsistency between the reserve system and the "pure and unhindered market" about which auction-house apologists love to boast. The reserve is designed to prevent bidders from getting bargains at the expense of consignors. It is also inconsistent with the role of the auctioneer, since he gets paid only if things sell, and therefore some galleries will not accept reserves. However, they are a dwindling number. In a consignor's market, with most galleries in desperate search for salable merchandise, most will agree to reasonable reserves.

There is, to be sure, a distinct down side to the system. If the reserves set are unrealistically high, many lots will fail to sell. It is not unusual now for the buy-in rate at large auction houses to run from 20 percent even to 40 percent. In fact, an auction that is 90 percent sold is regarded as a great triumph—a far cry from the days when everything found a buyer.

Finally, buyers should be aware of the absentee-bidding system. Every auction house of any size these days has procedures by which bidders may act without being present. Necessitated by the increasing number of buyers, many of whom may be located far from the gallery whose offerings they covet, and by the large number of auctions held on any given day, making it impossible for even the most nimble to be everywhere, absentee bidding is now a major factor in the auction game.

It works in this way: A potential buyer either views the merchandise prior to auction and then fills out a bid card stating the maximum figure he or she will pay for each item or he or she contacts the gallery, whose employees examine pieces the bidder is interested in, advise as to condition, and fill out the bid card in the buyer's behalf. The latter system, of course, assumes a situation of honesty and trust between buyer and gallery agent.

In either case, the absentee offers should be bid competitively; that is, in sequence, with bids coming from the floor. However, that is not always the case. Unscrupulous auctioneers may "throw in" an entire absentee bid to establish an artificially high opening or to spur other bidders on. Or, after other, "real" bidders have dropped out, the auctioneer may continue to offer your absentee bids against bids by his "shills" (see description later in this chapter) in the audience. Without being present it is often difficult to determine if your absentee bids are being properly handled, but if you find that you are consistently buying things at either your maximum figure or very close to it, it may be that the auctioneer is taking advantage of you.

One way to avoid this problem is through telephone bidding. All the major auction houses and an increasing number of regional galleries offer open telephone lines to important bidders, that is, those who either buy very expensive items or consistently buy large quantities. These lines are manned by gallery employees who act for the customers. Though not as good as being present, this system is superior to the use of absentee bids, since you can follow the bidding and perhaps even learn who your competitors are.

Choosing an Auction Gallery

It is seldom difficult to locate the auction galleries in your area. Auctioneers advertise widely—in local and regional newspapers, in the antiques trade papers, and even through the medium of handbills or flyers. However, not all auction houses are equal, and you will want to find the one or ones best suited to your needs.

If you are a specialist dealer—toys, guns, dolls, or nautical memorabilia, for example—you may find that most nearby auctions offer little of quality in your line. You may decide to travel to the infrequent specialized auctions in your field or to leave absentee bids.

Most dealers, though, will find what they want nearby. The next question is, what kind of management are you dealing with? Do they sell fresh merchandise from estates, or do they recycle dealer castoffs? Do they represent their offerings accurately? Do they treat bidders fairly, or do they utilize false bids, shills, and other devices to increase prices?

There is only one way to find out. Go to an auction but not to buy. Take along a flyer or advertisement, and compare the descriptions on it with the actual merchandise being offered. Are the "eighteenth-century chairs" really of the period? Is condition as described, and is everything advertised actually there? One well-known auction trick is to list important pieces to draw in the crowd and then announce that they have been "withdrawn" before the sale starts. Another thing to watch for is the term "with additions" in advertising. That usually means dealer leavings.

Mingle with the crowd and ask people what they think of the auctioneer. Does he seem honest, knowledgeable, and competent? If they are dealers, are they usually able to sell what they buy here at a profit? Not everyone will tell you the truth, of course, but you should get some flavor of the gallery.

The Viewing

Once you have decided the auction house is for you, the next step is to plan your bidding. Central to this is the viewing or auction preview, a period of a few hours to some days before the auction, during which you can examine the lots to be offered.

Anyone who bids without previously going over the pieces he or she is interested in is very foolish. The auctioneer has no obligation to describe anything he sells, is protected by law from liability for all but the most outrageous exaggerations (anything else is acceptable "puffing"), and in many cases may not even have looked at the lots. Nor can you hope to learn much about a piece during the two or three minutes that it may be held up for public scrutiny before the bidding begins.

On the other hand, viewing should tell you all you need to know to bid intelligently. But come equipped. You should have a magnifying glass (to look at hard-to-read pottery and silver marks), a magnet (to determine metal content), a flashlight (many auction storage rooms have insufficient lighting), a black light (useful in checking for overpainting in oils and hidden repairs on glass and pottery), and a measuring tape (to determine if that sofa you love will fit into your truck or through your door!). And, of course, you will need a pen or pencil and a pad of paper on which to note your comments.

If the auction house publishes a catalog with detailed descriptions of the things to be sold or, more often, a lot list that just shows the order in which items will be offered, you should have this as well. Sometimes catalogs and lot lists will contain estimates, which are guesses by the gallery staff as to the prices the lots will bring at auction. Anyone who has ever perused published auction results comparing them with preauction estimates for the same items will see why I call them "guesses." Even where based (as they generally are) on previous auction results for similar objects, estimates cannot account for such variables as bidding wars between antagonistic collectors, changes in collector taste, and the like. Nevertheless, these guesses have to be taken into consideration when planning your bids, because reserves, where present, are traditionally figured at or just below the low estimate. Thus, you know that you will have to go at least that high to prevent a buy-back.

You should begin your auction preview with a general walk

around, spotting the items you are most interested in (you may already have noted these in the catalog or auction advertising). Now concentrate on these. Examine each piece carefully; look for repairs, reconstructions, and additions. Don't be afraid to turn things upside down, pull out drawers, and remove covers, as long as you do these things carefully. You are entitled to check the merchandise, and any auctioneer who won't allow it probably has something to hide.

Particularly fragile objects should be stored in cases, and gallery personnel should be present to assist you in perusing these. You can also ask these people questions about the items to be sold, but bear in mind that they are in the business of selling. It won't be easy to get negative comments out of them. In most cases you are on your own.

What you have learned about each piece you wish to bid on should be noted on your pad or on the catalog along with the highest amount you will pay. This proposed bid should be based not only on your observation of the lot but also on your knowledge of what you can get for it at wholesale and retail. If you lack this information, obtain it from a price guide, another dealer, or some other source. Otherwise, you are flying blind!

Bidding

Once you have examined the lots to be sold and determined what you will pay for them, you are ready for the auction. In larger galleries you will be required to register with the management and obtain a bidding number through which your purchases will be identified. In some cases, you will be required to buy a catalog or to pay a (usually refundable) deposit in order to gain admission to the auction hall. Time was when auctions, especially in rural areas, were regarded as a form of community event to which all were invited. Today, auction is

big business and few owners want to see children or impecu-
nious oldsters in their halls. They want the seats filled with
well-to-do bidders!

There are a lot of little things that contribute to doing well
at an auction. One is where you sit. Down front is where the
"fat cats" go so that they can be seen and the high prices they
pay duly appreciated. That's not the spot for most dealers. Find
yourself a niche far enough back so that you can see where other
bids are coming from and where it will be harder for competitors to see if you are bidding (some even hide behind poles and
in doorways to obtain anonymity). You might even choose to
bid by a signal (such as raising your hat or touching your elbow)
that you can prearrange with the auctioneer. Why all the
secrecy? Because, in many cases, you don't want people to
know where you have obtained your merchandise and, particularly, what you have paid for it.

If you have, as I suggested, spent a night observing the
auctioneer, you may already have some idea of how he works
the crowd. That can be very helpful. Good auctioneers are good
psychologists. They try to incite avarice and competitiveness
among the audience while at the same time keeping them
relaxed and in good humor with a string of jokes.

Your goal, as a bidder, is to remember always that this is
business, not a contest or an amusement. The most fundamental rule for success is *never deviate from the top bid you have
set for yourself.* You decided on that figure while examining the
piece in a calm and dispassionate manner and with the best
knowledge available to you. It is hardly likely that you will
suddenly acquire some new insight in the heat of battle and
while seated fifty to a hundred feet from where the lot is being
displayed. However, a smart auctioneer can get an audience so
stirred up that people will, against their best judgment, make
bids that have little or no relationship to the market value of
what is on the block. Don't let this happen to you.

The keystone of the bidding is often the opening. The

auctioneer will call for a high bid, relative to value, hoping to get things moving at a point above the low estimate. Smart bidders will sit mute, forcing him to steadily reduce his demands until a realistic opening figure is reached. Thereafter, bids will be accepted in increments appropriate to the ultimate value of the lot. For example, a piece estimated at $100 to $150 should be bid up by $5 or $10 advances; an estimate of $2,000 would warrant advances of $100 or $150. Many auctioneers will refuse smaller sums on more valuable consignments.

You need not, however, follow the traditional sequence. There are several forms of strategic bidding. You may open with an extremely high bid (let us say $300 on a lot estimated at $500 to $650) or you may come in late on the bidding, which has been advancing in $10 jumps, with a $200 advance. In either case, the idea is to blow the opposition away, to make them feel that they cannot compete with you; in either case you, naturally, do not plan to go above your preset limit. But the opposition doesn't know that!

Don't assume that such ploys will always work. You aren't the only one familiar with them. On the other hand, they will keep both the auctioneer and competing bidders off balance, and they may enable you to "steal" some lots. But the competition is pretty sharp, too. Watch where the auctioneer is getting his bids. If you don't see any hands or bidding paddles as he calls out the advances, he may be "taking them off the wall"—making up fictitious bids. Some years ago, the chief auctioneer of one of the most prestigious eastern auction galleries was accused of pointing to various areas of the hall and pretending to take bids where, in fact, there were no bidders. Auctioneers may also pretend to have absentee bids or even telephone bidders when, in fact, the only person bidding is the one in the gallery who is being deceived.

Perhaps the best-known auction gimmick is the "shill." This is an auction-house employee who sits in the audience and bids against customers. The shill, of course, will not be someone you recognize as working for the company (auctioneers aren't stupid), but you may be able to spot the shill from a pattern of purchases. If someone seems to be bidding on a quantity of very different things (rugs, pottery, jewelry, furniture, and so on) he or she may be a shill.

Bear in mind that the shill's goal is to run the other bidders up, not to buy things. Sometimes his or hers will be the last bid. When that happens, the shill will loudly protest that the final bid was a "mistake," and the auctioneer will quickly award the lot to the underbidder, often mildly admonishing the shill to "pay attention next time." If this happens more than once with the same individual at an auction, you probably have a shill.

You may also be up against a "pool," a group of dealers who have agreed not to bid against each other in an attempt to keep prices artificially low and who are prone to "run up" other bidders to frighten them out of the bidding. Pooling, which was traditionally most evident in the rug and jewelry fields, has become less popular recently due to actions brought against several prominent dealers under the Sherman Antitrust Act. Technically, pooling may be a violation of the antitrust laws, but it certainly pales into insignificance alongside insider trading and other corrupt practices regularly indulged in by American corporations. On the other hand, antiques dealers are easy prey, while corporate officers are well insulated politically and economically.

In any case, you should not be concerned with either the auctioneer's bid rigging or the pool's antics *as long as you don't go above your bid limit.* Let them run you up. If you get the lot below your limit you will make money. If you stop there, the pool will pay top dollar, or the auctioneer will end up with an unsold lot (assuming he is using fictitious bids or an employee shill against you). They won't like you, but they will respect you.

Paying Up

Bidding can be fast and furious (indeed, the auctioneer prefers it to be), and when the hammer falls on your bid you own the merchandise. That is something to keep in mind. It means that a legal transaction has taken place, and if you have any second thoughts about the wisdom of your purchase, you may have to explain them to a judge. It also means that any damage your purchases may hereafter suffer (even though still on the premises) are your responsibility (subject, of course, to any cause of action for negligence you might have against someone, including the auctioneer's agents, causing the damage).

In most cases, your purchases are recorded under your bidding number by the gallery staff, and when you are ready to leave you go to them to settle up. You should, however, have determined previously what form of payment is accepted. All auction houses take cash or travelers' checks, and some have provisions for payment by VISA or MasterCard. Personal checks are another matter. Most auctioneers can tell horror stories about bad checks and, understandably, most will not accept them without a bank letter of credit or without having previously done business with the buyer. Don't be embarrassed. Find out in advance.

If you have made large purchases, you should also find out about shipping arrangements. Many small galleries (especially those conducting on-site auctions) insist that everything be removed on the day of the auction, but larger galleries will often allow you to store things for a few days. Also, these can often recommend shippers.

In every case where you deal with public carriers, be sure that you have a written contract of carriage, that hours of delivery are arranged in advance (some carriers are not above dumping a valuable cupboard on your front lawn if you aren't at home), and, most important, that you have adequate insurance coverage. Don't assume that the trucker will have insurance, even for its own negligence; pay for and provide it for yourself.

As you can see, buying at auction takes both knowledge and self-control. Nevertheless, it remains one of the major sources of merchandise for the antiques and collectibles dealer. Indeed, few dealers can afford to ignore the auction system. Even more, those dealers who learn to play the game wisely find auctions both pleasant and profitable.

6.

BUYING FROM OTHER DEALERS

Anyone who has been in the antiques field for any length of time comes to realize that other dealers make up a large portion of the market. Back when I was doing shows, I kept track of who my buyers were for a year and found out that seventy-eight percent of them had resale numbers, which means that they were, at least to some extent, "in the business." Of course, some collectors obtain resale certificates just to get discounts and avoid paying state sales taxes, but such a high percentage cannot be explained away solely in this manner. Dealers do buy from dealers—and with good reason.

In the first place, shops and shows are the most common media through which antiques and collectibles are exchanged. If sales have been good and the shop is looking bare, chances are that you will turn to your fellow dealers for replenishment. Auctions may be few and far between and subject to the uncertainties of collector-induced high prices, while getting into private homes can be difficult. But the dealer is always there.

Moreover, we all speak a more or less common language. There is a certain understanding about the nature, history, and quality of the merchandise, so that buying can be both pleasurable and financially rewarding. What one can't sell, another can.

But there are many dealers out there, and everyone has limited time, patience, and energy. In order to conduct a successful buying trip, you must organize it in such a way as to spend as much time as possible in the shops that both carry the type of goods you want and will sell them to you at a price that allows for a substantial profit.

To some, at least, the latter proposition may seem unlikely. If dealer prices tend over time to become uniform, how is it possible, you might ask, to buy favorably from someone else in the business? Part of the answer is the dealer's discount. Most dealers give a ten to fifteen percent discount off the retail price to others in the field. Thus, if you find in another store a fine country sawbuck table that is priced at $1,500, you can probably own it for $150 or $225 less. In theory you would then sell it to a retail customer for $1,500 and take your profit.

Yet, even if you did this on a regular basis you would soon be operating at a loss. No one knowledgeable ties up over a thousand dollars to make $225 or less. When you buy from other dealers, the discount is or should be a minor consideration. What is important is the price. If a piece has been marked well under *your* market value (again, you must know what similar objects bring in your local area), you can turn it over at a handsome profit even without a discount. The discount should just be icing on the cake!

What you are relying upon is 1) your greater knowledge and 2) market variations. As to the former, all antiques and collectibles dealers are not created equal. If you "do your homework" and learn to recognize the fine, the rare, and the valuable, you will soon realize that you are a member of a relatively small group. Many dealers, sad to say, treat everything (especially if it is not something they have a personal collector's interest in) as "merch" to be sold as quickly as possible for a minuscule markup. By gaining a sophisticated knowledge of antiques and collectibles you will be able to profit by their mistakes.

Concerning the latter, market variations, things that bring very little in one area of the country may do very well elsewhere. A sharp dealer will seek out early Empire furniture in the Midwest or in New Hampshire, where it has limited appeal, and sell it in New Orleans or Savannah, where there is a booming market. French bronzes, which are ignored in a Maine or Indiana shop, will ring the bell in New York or Los Angeles.

Do not assume that these price differentials reflect simply the ignorance of provincial dealers. You will find knowledgeable antiques and collectibles authorities in every area of the country. It is simply that in certain areas certain things bring very little. Even if one is aware of higher prices elsewhere, lack of contacts may prevent obtaining these more elevated figures. By establishing contact with a dealer who lacks an outlet, you will benefit both yourself, by obtaining a source, and this dealer, by providing him or her with a new market.

The Picker-Dealer

Finding regional sources is not always easy, but one type of dealer will usually find you: this is the picker-dealer. "Pickers," as they are known to the trade, are antiques wholesalers, people who prefer to spend most of their time looking for bargains at auctions, estate sales, in private homes—wherever something good can be bought below retail. They then sell these items to retail dealers rather than to the general public. If you have an open shop or advertise in the trade publications, sooner or later a picker will seek you out. A loaded truck may pull up in front of the store, or you might get a call from someone wanting to know if you are buying porcelain or quilts or architectural items.

Don't make the mistake of assuming that the picker is a bumpkin with a load of junk out of his grandfather's barn. He or she is probably a very sharp professional. After all, he or she has chosen to sell to dealers, who may be assumed to know something of the trade and values. You sell to members of the public, who in most cases know much less.

However, quick turnover is the secret of the picker's trade, and in order to move things rapidly it is necessary to sell at figures substantially below retail. Most wholesalers will let things go for forty to sixty percent of what you would expect a customer to pay. They can afford to do this because of their sources. They are, if successful, buying at a fraction (sometimes no more than ten percent) of market value. They will not, of course, disclose these sources, but you benefit from their knowledge by way of lower prices.

Pickers, though, are not the ultimate solution to buying problems. Good ones are hard to find and harder to keep. If they have really good "merch" at rock-bottom prices, they will have lots of places to sell it. You will be competing with many other dealers. Moreover, care should always be used in dealing with anyone who shows up at your door with merchandise to sell. Many pickers seem to have no permanent address, out-of-state license plates, and readily forgettable names. Anyone buying from them should get a completely descriptive receipt that includes a checkable address. Some identification, such as a driver's license, is also helpful.

If you feel uncomfortable about asking for these things, you may explain that they are required because of your state's tough laws governing the selling of stolen property; but the laws are for your protection as well. Some pickers handle stolen goods; others are not above selling fakes, altered pieces of furniture, and the like. Don't let your desire to buy what appear to be great bargains blind you to the fact that you may have a hard time tracking down your picker if something turns out to be not what it was represented to be.

Seeking Out Dealers

Pickers will not begin to supply enough merchandise for a growing business. You must also find other antiques and collectibles dealers who have things you can buy at a profit. For starters, canvass local shops. Many dealers have a circuit they cover enabling them to survey their competitors' new acquisitions on a weekly or biweekly basis. Chances are you already know who the community dealers are but, if not, a quick check in the Yellow Pages, the newspapers, and whatever antiques tabloid covers your area should enable you to locate most of them.

After a few trips back you will begin to see that, while most shops rarely have anything you want at prices you can afford, there are a few that seem to share your interests and to offer an opportunity to buy well. These are the ones deserving of your attention. You may visit them twice a week and the others only twice a month, or you may even call their proprietors every few days to check on new acquisitions. If possible, encourage them to contact you when something in your line comes in. Many dealers are glad to have a ready outlet; others, though, are not willing to play favorites or are simply too lazy to pick up the telephone. In any case, always make some attempt to establish a special relationship.

Eventually, you may find that local dealers are not enough to provide you with the variety and quantity you require. You will have to cast your net farther.

The Buying Trip

Magic words, "the buying trip," promising a combination of vacation and business venture replete with tax deductions for practically everything, mad on-the-road adventures in the best tradition of Jack Kerouac, and, in the end, a lot of wonderful fresh merchandise bought at low, country prices.

Were it only so simple! Any fruitful buying trip, whether a day to nearby towns or a week spent in New England or down through the Appalachians, is usually the result of careful planning. If you just hop into the car and wander around the countryside looking for signs that say "Antiques Shop," you are going to do a lot of driving and not much buying.

There are several ways to learn about antiques shops in distant areas. One of the best is through the antiques tabloids. *Antique Review, Antiques and the Arts Weekly, Maine Antique Digest,* and other regional publications contain advertisements from hundreds of dealers throughout the nation. More important, groups of antiques-shop owners, such as county dealers' associations, will often run joint advertisements providing a map showing locations of their members, hours of business, and areas of specialization.

Other ways to locate potential targets include collecting dealers' cards at shows and flea markets, checking the Yellow Pages advertisements in telephone directories from distant eas, and just asking collectors and dealers where they like to buy in California, Wisconsin, or wherever you plan to head.

Once you are armed with a handful of leads, decide upon the best time to go. Of course, those who must travel only on weekends or during a summer vacation are limited; but if possible, choose your period carefully.

Some prefer the off-season. For example, they shop New England and the Midwest during the late fall, winter, and early spring, when business is slow and open-handed tourists few. March and April can be especially fruitful, as local dealers have been stocking up at country auctions and may be pinched by tax bills. On the other hand, Florida and the deep South are often best during the summer, when the heat wilts local buyers' enthusiasm. At any rate, don't hesitate to go against the grain; that is, look for your treasures in the areas where they are least likely to be appreciated. Ask for Russian icons and Japanese netsuke in Maine shops featuring painted furniture and quilts; ask for period pewter in a doll shop. You will be amazed at how much you will find and how inexpensive it may be. All dealers buy households or large lots in order to get certain things they are especially interested in. The rest of the merchandise often just sits around or is sold cheaply to the first lucky inquirer.

Once you have decided on a time, call ahead! Posted hours seem to mean little to many dealers, particularly in the off-season. Once you have driven twenty miles out of your way to find a closed shop, you will appreciate the wisdom of making appointments. Sure, it costs more in telephone charges, but it also cuts down on mileage, frustration, and dead time on the road. It may also induce dealers to save something special for you.

Try to cram as many stops into the day as time and your temperament allow. Some dealers eat on the road and fly through shops in no time flat. Others prefer a leisurely lunch and careful examination of the merchandise. Generally, specialist dealers can cover the most territory, because their needs (antique guns or Shaker furniture, for example) are so specific that they can cover most stops quickly. If you, like me, buy a lot of different things, it will take you longer to cover your route.

Negotiation

Dealing with other dealers is different from buying at auction or from the general public. In most cases, you share a somewhat similar background and knowledge, so that much of the preliminary conversation can be bypassed. You are there to buy.

They want to sell. You both (hopefully) know the merchandise and its approximate value. If your valuations are more or less in accord or they think the things you want are worth less than you do (oh, happy chance!), you will do business. How this business will be conducted is another matter.

I have always found that respect is the best policy. No matter how small or insignificant a shop may be or how seemingly ignorant its proprietor may appear, you should behave just as you would wish to be treated by a potential buyer. Don't start off by running down the merchandise or showing your superior knowledge (in fact, if in your possession, that advantage should be concealed). A friendly, open approach is usually best. Most dealers will, where possible, tell you what they know about the background of a piece, and that is a legitimate query. Even if you can see no repairs or restorations, ask if there are any; and of course examine each prospective acquisition with care.

Assemble your purchases in groups so as to be able to seek a package discount. Where most dealers will only give ten to fifteen percent off on a single item, the prospect of a large sale will often cause them to bend a bit. Don't be afraid to ask. With rare exceptions, a dealer will not be offended by a polite request for greater leeway on the price. After all, he or she would do the same. It is at this point one also raises the question of restoration or damage. A sharp dealer will point out that this is already reflected in the asking price, but a surprisingly large number will lower the ante at this point. The important thing is to broach the issue in a nonthreatening way.

Once you have "scoped out" the shop and selected what you want, ask the proprietor if he or she has anything else in the line you are interested in. Dealers seldom have everything on view. They may be refinishing a piece, not have room for it, or be a little reluctant to part with it just now. There is nothing like the prospect of a sale to flush out the treasures.

Payment is the next step. Cash is often preferred, and an

offer to pay cash may be a lever toward obtaining an even lower price. However, this should never be at the expense of obtaining a detailed written receipt. This is always critical. Without a receipt you have no proof that you legitimately acquired your purchases, and little recourse if you want to return something. Some dealers take credit cards, but often these people will (due to the finance charge involved) give smaller dealer's discounts. In most cases, a check is the answer. Be prepared with adequate identification, especially on out-of-state and large transactions. If you are really buying "big-ticket" items, a current bank letter of credit is a handy thing to carry. Otherwise, you may find that sellers will insist on calling your bank or holding the merchandise until the check clears. Wouldn't you?

One more thing about the receipt. If the dealer has represented a piece in a specific way—"This is an 18th-c. Chippendale chair," for example—ask him or her to put that down on the receipt. Such a statement constitutes an express warranty and will make it much easier to get your money back if a piece turns out to be not as described.

Shipping may become a factor where purchases are too large to be taken with you. Unless you have already made your own shipping arrangements, you may have to ask the dealer about this. She or he has no obligation in this matter, and any shipping would normally be at your expense. On the other hand, if you sense an eagerness to get rid of a larger piece, you may even be able to work shipping into the deal. Remember, there are no real limits to negotiations among dealers.

On the other hand, if the seller does undertake shipping, either at his or her cost or yours, be sure that he or she has written instructions as to where and when to deliver, how the piece is to be packed, and, most important, insurance coverage. *Never* ship anything of value without having it insured.

A final gesture before departing: leave your business card

with a suggestion that the store owner call you collect if anything in your line comes in. Of course, most won't; but every
so often you will be pleasantly surprised. Establishing relationships with good, preferably out-of-the-way, sources will go
a long way toward giving your shop that "always fresh" look all
dealers and customers crave.

7

BUYING FROM PRIVATE PARTIES

*O*ne of the most tantalizing and frustrating aspects of the dealer's life is buying from "privates," nonprofessional owners of antiques and collectibles. At one extreme, it is the hope of every person in the field to get into that old house or attic stuffed full of "fresh merch," all offered at ludicrously low prices. On the other hand, there is the realization that such treasure troves are difficult to come by. Even the definition of who is a private party is subject to question, since it may include not only the little old lady with the bulging attic but also highly professional tag-sale experts whom she may hire to handle a sale of her home's contents or the people who run church and other nonprofit sales and bazaars.

In general, a private may be defined as someone who does not buy and sell antiques as a business, either full- or part-time. Implicit in this is the idea that he or she will consequently be either unaware or less aware of prices in the field and more likely to sell far below the going rate—hence, the obvious attraction for the dealer.

Professional Tag Sales

Over the past decade there has grown up, particularly in the well-to-do suburbs of large cities, a class of entrepreneurs specializing in the dispersal of estates and household contents. Inevitably, antiques and collectibles will be involved in some of these sales, but such sales cover a far broader range of objects—everything from household appliances and automobiles to mountains of used clothing.

Knowledge of price and quality, as well as the basic recognition of what an antique is, vary greatly among those who run tag sales. Some organizers make a serious effort to learn the field or may have themselves been in the business. Others understand nothing or have advanced little beyond recognizing the difference between sterling and silver plate. The latter are, of course, particularly popular among dealers, and long lines await the opening of their every sale.

Whatever the state of their knowledge and wherever in the country they may be based, tag-sale people operate in more or less the same manner. Understanding this modus operandi will enable the dealer to buy to best advantage.

First, the people running such sales either buy the contents outright and then sell them on their own behalf or, more often, work on a commission, usually twenty-five to fifty percent of the total sales. In either case, the contents of many homes simply do not generate enough in sales to make a professional tag sale profitable. Consequently, you can usually figure that if professionals are involved there may be something of value in the house; and that often means antiques or collectibles. The question is how to get your hands on them.

The usual manner, though not always the best, is to check your local newspapers (usually starting on a Wednesday, as most sales are held Thursday through Sunday) for sale announcements. Some will mention the antiques being sold, or even give a complete list of what is for sale. If there is a telephone number provided, call up and try to get a description of what is available. Some dealers will even go to a sale site and peer through windows (assuming, as is usually the case, that the house is unoccupied), trying to see what is being offered. This latter technique is not recommended. You might get arrested or even shot at as a trespasser!

It is important to determine, if possible, just what sort of "antiques" or collectibles are being offered. In many areas the potential buyer is confronted with a choice among several sales occurring at about the same time (usually 9:00 or 10:00 A.M. through 4:00 P.M.) on the same day. Most sales will have nothing of value. You want to go to the right place. Moreover, the definition of antique used by many tag-sale operators is extremely generous. By calling, you may learn that the ". . . fine eighteenth-century Chippendale tea table . . ." being offered is really a twentieth-century reproduction.

Having made your choice of sales, you must now deal with the rules of the game. Most sophisticated tag-sale operatives work on a numbers system. People arriving at a sale are given consecutive numbers and admitted in order of their appearance. Both fire laws and the orderly conduct of a sale make it impractical to admit everyone at once. At a good sale, dozens of people may be lined up several hours before opening. They may have worked out an informal numbering arrangement, which is later honored by the tag-sale staff, who usually start doling out numbers an hour prior to start of the sale.

However, the more aggressive dealers have been at work long before this. Where the possibility of a real bonanza exists they—or, more often, teenagers in their hire—may have been positioned before the house in the wee hours of the night. Or they may simply arrive a few minutes before opening and buy a front runner's number for as much as a thousand dollars.

But being first in line isn't enough. You must also know what you are looking at and be able to make split-second decisions as to quality and salability. When the doors open, there is little time for reflection. Tag sales are a combination of an obstacle-course race and guerrilla warfare. A sharp dealer will have printed stickers with his or her name and address and the word SOLD someplace extremely handy, usually affixed loosely to a sleeve so that they quickly can be removed and slapped on desired pieces as the dealer hurries through the house. And make sure the labels are hard to remove. Some of your competitors (you will soon learn who they are) are not above pulling off your labels and substituting their own!

Mark or pick up everything you might possibly want. Later you can go back and decide if you really care to make the purchase. There is no time for that initially. To hesitate then is to lose. Tagging something with your sticker is not like bidding at an auction; you can always change your mind.

Paying for your purchases is usually fairly straightforward. The tag-sale staff will have set up a table near the exit at which they receive payment. In some cases, they may have a person in each room who will record what you buy within that area on a sales slip, which you then present at the check-out table. This facilitates the often tedious process of payment—an important consideration since many customers want to get on to the next sale.

Pricing of antiques and collectibles at professional tag sales is customarily on a wholesale basis; in other words, you pay what you might when buying from another dealer. However, few tag-sale people are as knowledgeable as dealers; and you may find things that are greatly underpriced. Moreover, most such sales are undertaken on a "broom clean" basis, which obligates the operator to empty the house at the end of the one- to three-day sales period. The consequent pressure to dispose of everything makes most sellers amenable to discounts. Sometimes you can get a reduction just by asking for it (particularly if you are a dealer well-known to the staff); more often you can leave a "bid," a figure you will pay if the piece does not sell for the asking price. Soon after noon on the last day of the sale the staff will examine their bid list and notify the successful buyers.

While this is the general procedure, there are other ways to play the tag-sale game. If you are known as a particularly heavy buyer, you may be admitted to a special "dealers' preview" the day before the house is opened to the public. Such events are kept quiet since uninvited dealers and the general public are understandably hostile to the idea, and many tag-sale operatives will not conduct them. Moreover, discounts are seldom given at a preview, and in some cases sharp tag-sale staffs will actually raise prices, hoping that in their "feeding frenzy" the dealers will not notice. This is a dangerous practice, though, since dealers are extremely important to the success of any good tag sale. They buy most of the antiques and collectibles.

There is another way into the tag sale—through the back door. As previously mentioned, most tag-sale managers lack the expertise of antiques dealers. After learning belatedly (some never learn!) that they have sold a thousand-dollar item for twenty dollars, they will often accept a dealer's offer to appraise the antiques and collectibles in a house before they are offered to the public. This arrangement may be on a paid basis (in which case the appraiser at least gets to see the contents first) or as part of a deal enabling the appraiser to buy prior to public sale. The latter is usually more desirable and, indeed, just, since the dealer's appraisals are usually raising the prices he or she must pay. It also creates a conflict of interest if one is both appraising and buying. But there are no legal objections to such an arrangement, provided the owner of the goods has consented to it.

However one may approach them, professionally run tag sales are on the increase throughout the United States and Canada; and they offer one of the last places where dealers may obtain truly fresh merchandise. Of course, this is always subject to the possibility that a sale may be "salted" with excess dealer merchandise or things the tag-sale operator couldn't sell at a prior event.

Private Tag Sales

Far more numerous than professionally run sales are the barn, yard, garage, or house sales conducted weekly throughout the United States and Canada. These run into the millions each year and have become so numerous in some areas that local governments have been forced to enact zoning laws against the traffic and noise nuisance they may create. State sales-tax authorities wrestle with legislation designed to get them a piece of the money that changes hands, and both auctioneers and antiques dealers lament the competition they provide. But such sales can also be a source of fresh merchandise for the dealer and in some cases offer an entry into private homes and collections.

Superficially, professional and private tag sales are much alike. Both offer a mixed bag of everything from used household goods to antiques. There are marked differences, though. Most professionals must have at least some general knowledge of antiques and their values. Few householders do. This can lead to incredible buys. Those stories about Tiffany lamps being purchased for five dollars and Lalique vases going for fifty cents are true!

On the other hand, where almost all professional sales must have something of value (though it may not be old) to justify their existence, the vast majority of private sales offer nothing of any interest to the dealer. That means that much time will be wasted chasing the pot of gold at the end of this rainbow.

Moreover, crowd control is seldom a priority at the private sales. Numbers aren't usually given out, and even if a sale is scheduled for 9:00 A.M., the chances are the owners will be selling an hour or so earlier if buyers start showing up. That means you cannot rely on printed timetables. If a sale looks good, go at the crack of dawn and knock on the door. Also, unlike the professionals, who seldom buy such stories, you can sometimes call a private or go to the house a day early on some pretense (a trip out of town, a doctor's appointment, or some such) and get in before the crowd. Remember, most are only concerned with selling, not the rules of the game as observed by dealers and professional tag-sale staffs.

Since in most American communities anywhere from twenty to a hundred tag sales are taking place each week (usually between Thursday and Sunday), one must be selective and plan the day's activities with care.

RULE #1: Acquire a detailed street map of the area. Don't rely on your memory or count on others to direct you. Time is of the essence.

RULE #2: Plan where you are going before you get in the car. Tag-sale notices appear in local newspapers; on bulletin boards; at places like the post office, supermarket, and town hall; and may be found nailed to trees and telephone poles throughout the community. Always check the dates. It is both embarrassing and a waste of time to show up for a sale that was held last week!

Assemble the notices and separate out those that look interesting. Key words are "estate," "property in family thirty years," "old barn contents," and, of course, "antiques." To be avoided are sales boasting "new" or "nearly new" items, "baby clothes," and so forth. That is certainly not to say that you will never find anything of value among such offerings. It is possible, but time is of the essence, and you must spend it in the most likely places.

Arrange the sales in order of desirability and then mark

their locations on your map. Ideally, the potentially most productive would be in the same neighborhoods. They won't be. You will have to make some tough choices, but what you must avoid is running back and forth across town. Try to select a group of five or six sales in one area and then a similar cluster in another adjacent location. If you cut down travel time you may be able to do several dozen sales in a day.

RULE #3: Be fast and sure. Once on the scene, buying techniques are fairly simple. As most of the things displayed will be of no interest to you, you can go through the yard, barn, or house quickly. I recommend a brisk walk; running is unseemly. Pick up *everything* you have the slightest interest in, priced or not. Think of the sale as a supermarket. If you don't want it you can always put an item back. If you pause to debate the matter, someone will snatch it away.

Collect your treasures and take them to whoever is handling the cashbox. In most cases, don't try to bargain unless encouraged by signs ("Ask for a better price," "We like to haggle") or the seller's attitude. Remember, most people who run these sales are experienced only with the general retail world. They wouldn't dream of asking for a better price on gasoline or a pair of shoes, and they may be offended by aggressive discounting. Besides, in most cases the prices asked will probably be well below wholesale. If you have a real problem with a price, approach the matter of a compromise in a delicate manner.

RULE #4: Check out the hidden assets. Once you have paid for your goodies (usually in cash—and don't expect in most cases to get a receipt; they may think you are from the IRS), ask if the proprietors have anything else they would like to sell. Bear in mind that they probably know little of antiques and collectibles and never dreamed that those old hooked rugs on the floor or ratty-looking baskets in the attic could be of any interest to anyone. A few key questions may put you on to a lot of things you might otherwise miss. Try things like, "Do you have any old tables or cupboards in blue or red paint?" "Do you have any old oil lamps in the barn?" "Do you have any colored glass?" If you get any sort of encouraging answer, try to arrange to see the pieces. Getting in the door is the key to good buying!

Charity Sales

A wide variety of organizations, from the Salvation Army to local churches, synagogues, hospitals, fire departments, and so forth, either maintain thrift or consignment shops or hold periodic sales at which donated articles are sold to raise money for the charity.

These shops and sales may provide a limited source for dealers in antiques and collectibles. The reason that I say "limited" is that it is well-known in the trade that nearly all such outlets have a connection with an antiques dealer or knowledgeable collector who either buys anything of value that passes through the door or prices the pieces in such a way that they are offered at retail or high wholesale values. Consequently, few knowledgeable dealers spend much time at professional outlets run by charitable organizations.

Church bazaars or "white elephant" sales are something else again. These are often organized by amateurs, who may lack professional guidance. Your best bets are sales in the inner city and in rural areas. Suburban organizations are much more likely to be aware of antiques and collectibles values.

In any case, the rule is, as always, get there early. The more likely the sale, the more competitors there will be in line. If you have a connection in the sponsoring organization, try to get in early. Best of all, become the dealer who "skims" the merchandise before it is offered for sale.

The Private Owner

Dealing with nonprofessionals who are offering antiques and collectibles for sale is superficially attractive, but it has some serious practical and ethical aspects. In the first place, there is the practical problem of finding sellers. The so-called "door-knocker" picker resolves this by literally going house to house, particularly in rural areas, asking if people have any "old things" to sell. Most dealers lack the time to do this, and many don't have the stomach for it.

There are other ways. If you run an open shop you will find that people will bring things to you. Sometimes these will be desirable in themselves. On other occasions you may decide to purchase something you don't greatly desire, because it may allow you access to other things the seller has.

Never let such a seller go without asking if he or she has other antiques or collectibles available for sale. And be specific. You are not talking to an antiques dealer or even the operator of a professional tag sale. Assume the person knows nothing at all about antiques, and describe what you want in detail. Don't just say, "Do you have any coverlets or folk art or porcelain?" Describe a coverlet, a weather vane, or a piece of Meissen. Many people own things that they consider to be of no value and would never offer for sale but which antiques dealers would love to get their hands on.

The same thing applies to advertising, the other way to reach potential sellers. If you are running an advertisement in the local newspaper, spell out what you are looking for. Ads simply asking for "antiques" or "old paintings" will seldom draw the kind of response you want. And for advertisements to be effective they must be targeted to your audience and they must catch the reader's eye. Use bold headings, DESPERATE FOR ANTIQUES, MONEY TO BURN, and the like, and change the copy every week or so. If an advertisement for Depression glass, bronzes, and jade gets no response, try one for Oriental rugs, old trains, and majolica. Keep changing until you hit on something your audience owns. Using the same old notice week after week shows a lack of imagination.

Be honest with people. Admit you are a dealer, rather than hiding behind the hoary "serious collector" gambit. Few people are naïve enough to buy this anyway, and if you begin to negotiate seriously with a potential seller, sooner or later you are going to compromise your story of being just a collector. At this point you will have cast doubts on your credibility, which may affect the whole future course of the transaction. It is much better to make it clear from the beginning that you are in business and must, therefore, make a profit.

Negotiation

Purchasing from a private party is often more complex than dealing with another dealer, a tag-sale operator, or an auctioneer. There is, initially, the problem of language. Since the private party lacks expertise in the areas of "merch," "discount," "deal," and the like, as well as a dealer's outlook on the objects, one must proceed slowly and explicitly. Price is a particularly touchy area.

Dealers can no longer assume that anything goes in negotiating with a potential seller. At least three recent legal cases, two of which remain undecided at this moment, cast an ominous specter over the dealer-seller relationship. The two pending cases, one in Vermont, the other in Massachusetts, involve superficially similar situations. In each, a seller is suing a dealer who bought something at a relatively modest price and then sold it later at a much higher one. In each, there are allegations of misrepresentation—that the dealer deliberately misled the owner as to the value of his possessions and as to what the dealer could obtain for them, thereby inducing the owner to sell for far less than the pieces were worth.

Regardless of how these cases may be resolved, it seems clear that a dealer who deliberately lies to someone in order to get them to sell something is running a risk of being sued if he or she later sells at a substantial profit. The first thing this should teach us is that in dealing with privates, the less said the better. Ideally, a transaction might go something like this: "Do you want to sell that?" "Yes." "How much?" "Ten dollars." "Fine, sold." Unfortunately, things are seldom so simple with private owners.

Many owners refuse to put a price on things, urging the dealer to name a price, since he or she ". . . knows so much more about what these things are worth." Where possible, avoid putting a price on things in this manner. In the first place, the owner may already have "shopped the item about" and gotten bids from several other dealers or checked out a price guide. Consequently, if he (or she) regards your offer as too low, he may be insulted and withdraw from further bargaining. If it is much more than he thought the object was worth, the offer may feed his fantasy of an even higher price. Either way, the dealer usually loses by quoting a price, unless the parties have a previous history of dealings and mutual trust. Also, in light of the pending lawsuits, an offer substantially below the going market value for an antique or collectible might be construed by some as a form of misrepresentation or fraud against the seller.

In the third suit, several years ago in the Canadian courts, the buyer successfully defended himself against the seller by convincing the court that he did not know how much the piece of furniture he bought was worth. Ignorance, which dealers should try to overcome, now becomes a necessity as a defense against claims of overreaching!

I must say that I find it remarkable that in a country where sharp dealing and astute use of superior knowledge form the basis for every industry from the stock market to real estate brokerage, there is in effect a movement afoot to deny the antiques professional the fruit of his or her years of study and experience. If a dealer must disclose to a nonprofessional seller all he or she knows about a piece and about its value in the marketplace in order to avoid a damaging lawsuit, the antiques world as we now know it will be greatly changed.

On the other hand, "puffing" and half-truths, which are common parlance in the auction world and among dealers, clearly should not be employed in dealing with privates. The dealer who utilizes such tactics not only subjects himself or herself to risk, he or she also adds support to the arguments calling for greater state or federal regulation of the antiques and art world.

Are there, then, only perils and no advantages in buying from private owners? Not so. Private collections remain the one great source of fresh merchandise—antiques and collectibles that have not been seen in shops for months or run through a half-dozen auctions. One must simply show caution and fairness in dealing with their owners.

One good general rule is not to sell in the same area where you buy. If you purchase something for thirty-five dollars from a neighbor and then put it in your shop priced at seventy dollars (a perfectly reasonable price in light of your overhead and profit margin), your seller may well hear about it. Since few non-dealers understand the differences between the antiques trade and other small businesses, he (or she) is likely to be offended. That means no more purchases either from him or anyone he tells the tale to. Discretion is the word here.

And, of course, it is just good business to treat your private sources fairly. Not only can they provide you with salable merchandise over a period of time (some dealers buy out of houses for years, often at tax time, when their purchases help to bridge the gap between social-security payments and mounting real estate costs) but also lead you to other willing sellers. In fact, if you scratch a top-notch picker, you will probably find underneath a man or woman who has a very good reputation in his or her community and loads of house calls to make each month. Despite the claims that everything has been dug out, there are still many attics, houses, and barns full of merchandise not yet picked over. You will find them if you deal with the privates.

8.

BUYING FROM FOREIGN
SOURCES

*D*uring the late 1970s and early '80s many American dealers began to buy heavily from English and Continental suppliers of antiques and collectibles. In so doing the American
dealers took advantage of a favorable rate of exchange and at the
same time satisfied two classes of customers: those interested
in formal French or English furniture and accessories and those
attracted to the so-called stripped pine imported from England
and Scandinavia and the Country French furnishings from
France.

While certainly affected by the decline of the dollar, this
trade continues today and is important enough to some dealers
that one should be somewhat familiar with the often complex
nature of the transactions involved.

In the first place, a dealer may either buy "on site" by
traveling to England or the Continent to select his or her own
purchases (something that some knowledgeable American
dealers have been doing for decades), or through a local agent
who will choose merchandise for shipment. Those who elect
the former course of action normally travel during the off-
season, November through March, when European dealers are
less busy and prices are not elevated for tourists. Some Amer-

ican buyers (especially the more experienced) prefer to travel and shop on their own, in which case they will probably have scheduled appointments in advance with dealers specializing in the things they are interested in.

If you are not familiar with the European market, however, you may spend a lot of time and money wandering the countryside trying to find things to buy. Continental dealers, especially, keep very irregular hours, and many do not advertise. Moreover, outside of the British Isles, France, and Italy, language barriers can be a problem. The dealers most likely to speak English are those offering inferior merchandise to tourists.

As a newcomer to foreign buying, it may be best for you to retain the services of a local antiquarian or antiques broker, who will direct you to shops where you can obtain what you seek, will bargain for you with dealers, and will generally attempt to make your buying trip a pleasant experience. People who provide such services often are listed in hotel directories and with tourist bureaus.

While it is true that some of these agents may be in cahoots with local dealers, receiving a fee for steering buyers to them, most depend primarily upon the fees paid by their customers (the amounts vary from country to country but are generally not unreasonable). Therefore such brokers are likely to serve you well, so that they can obtain both further business and favorable recommendations.

If you choose to operate on your own, you will probably want to frequent the large antiques bazaars found in London, Paris, Madrid, and other cultural centers. Some real bargains can still be found here, especially by those who have the stamina to get up early and walk for hours through the crowded stalls. Shopping in the countryside is much more chancy unless you are experienced or have a guide. Europe has far fewer open shops in small towns and rural areas than the United States does, and those that exist are often hard to locate. Wandering may appeal to some, but an itinerary with scheduled appointments will turn up the most merchandise in the least time.

Auction is really not an option for most American buyers, except in England, where Sotheby's, Christie's, Phillips, and several smaller London houses offer frequent and well-publicized sales. There are auctions in other major centers, such as Geneva, Paris, Hamburg, and Monte Carlo, but these occur infrequently and a trip would have to be structured around them. Moreover, such auctions are often designed primarily for local dealers (indeed, in Japan attendance is limited *only* to these), and it is difficult for an outsider to do well.

For those who choose not to travel, there are agencies that will buy for you. Typically, these are volume dealers who will choose a group of antiques and collectibles to be shipped by "container" or fraction thereof. Containers, which can be transported to the docks by truck, loaded aboard a ship, and then brought to your shop again by truck, measure 8 by 8.5 feet and are either 20 or 40 feet long. They have, over the past decade, become a favorite method of transporting bulk shipments of antiques, especially from Europe to the United States.

When buying a typical "blind container" (that is, one whose contents you have neither chosen nor inspected), you can expect to receive a mixture of furnishings: wardrobes, chests of drawers, chairs, tables, and the like in various woods, such as pine, oak, and mahogany. Unless you are willing to pay well above the going rate, all these will be either late Victorian or outright reproductions of earlier styles. If you desire, the package can include "smalls," such as pottery, glass, lamps, and an assortment of metalware. While nothing will be of much quality, the quantity will be sufficient to stock a small antiques shop for several months.

You can also have a reliable agent individually select better-quality antiques to fill your container. He or she will furnish you in advance with photographs and descriptions so that you may make a selection. Of course, you will pay more for such goods and for that kind of service.

European dealers and agents who pack and ship container loads of antiques and collectibles advertise in most major antiques publications both here and abroad. In larger European cities, they are also usually listed in the Yellow Pages of the telephone directory.

Those who make their own purchases abroad will want to enlist the assistance of a local packing and shipping firm to arrange the details of delivery to the United States. Such companies, most readily available in the British Isles but also found on the Continent and in Scandinavia, will not only arrange safe wrapping and transportation by air or sea but will also deal with such complexities as authentication of objects as antique so as to avoid United States customs duties (generally levied on anything less than a hundred years old), preparation of the numerous export documents required for shipment, and any problems that may arise under governmental regulations covering the export of state treasures.

The latter is an increasing problem for those buying fine art and better-quality antiques. Governments throughout Europe, Asia, and South America, concerned with the loss of important examples of the national patrimony, have passed statutes either forbidding the export of significant or historic works of art or (as is the case with England) established a waiting period prior to export during which organizations or individuals within the country are given an opportunity to buy back the pieces by meeting the purchaser's price.

One can hardly argue with the justice of such laws (how would we like it if the Japanese bought the Statue of Liberty or John Paul Jones's sword!), but some laws are so broad as to include, at least in theory, almost anything produced in a country.

There are two ways to deal with the problem. France and Mexico, among other nations, provide forms to their dealers in art and antiquities wherein they certify that a purchase is not a national treasure, a determination which, unless obviously false, is not usually challenged by governmental authorities. Whenever you buy anything of importance, always try to obtain such a document if available. If this procedure does not exist in the country where you are purchasing, or if you feel that the piece you are after is of sufficient importance to cause a problem, you will be well advised to retain a local agent or customs-house broker to guide your path through the potential mine field of governmental regulations.

Another matter to be concerned with when buying overseas is the quality of your purchases. Europeans and Asians have been reproducing their finest examples of art, furniture, silver, glass, and pottery for hundreds of years. The majority of what is available for export at reasonable prices is not of the period it imitates. Unless you are extremely knowledgeable, you will need expert guidance when buying abroad.

There are, of course, many American dealers who are not concerned with this. Three quarters of the "early nineteenth-century" stripped pine from England and Scandinavia that is sold in this country has been made up in the past ten years from old barn boards (if in doubt, look at the nails: the wire nails commonly found in these pieces were not available until the 1880s!). The same may be said of much of the French Provincial furniture sold here.

Further, most of the English mahogany offered by medium-range dealers and decorators, though in eighteenth-century styles, was actually manufactured circa 1870–1930 by highly competent copyists. Dealers, particularly in the Northeast and the South, may offer these pieces without making any distinction as to their period. If, however, you wish to handle *antiques*, you would be well advised to choose very carefully among the numerous items available either directly from Europe or through importers. If you don't, you may receive a rude surprise when your purchases pass through American customs:

While antiques are not subject to duty, later reproductions fall within the category of "wooden furniture" and are taxed at the same rate as brand-new household furnishings. Customs officers may not be authorities on antiques and collectibles, but they have seen a lot of reproductions.

Buying abroad is obviously quite different from buying here in the United States. If you want to do it, you must learn the rules and develop the necessary expertise. Otherwise, employ a trusted agent who can act on your behalf and guarantee that you get the quality for which you are paying.

9·

BUYING BY MAIL

Anyone glancing through the pages of a weekly or monthly antiques trade publication will immediately be struck by the dozens or even hundreds of individual dealer advertisements. These reflect the burgeoning antiques mail-order market. No longer content to sit in a shop waiting for business, merchants are reaching out across the nation seeking new sources of supply as well as new sales outlets.

Mail-order antiques buying can make sense for a dealer, particularly if he or she is living in an area of the country where local supplies of desired merchandise are hard to come by—for example, if you have chosen to concentrate on early American furniture and related accessories such as baskets, woodenware, ceramics, and coverlets but are located on the West Coast or in New Orleans. With the increasing enthusiasm for "country style," collectors and decorators throughout the United States are more and more interested in such objects. However, in many localities estate and house sales will yield little in this line. Dealers must either embark on expensive and time-consuming buying trips to the East or Midwest or rely on haulers who will charge a premium for goods the quality of which one has little control over.

Another type of dealer for whom mail-order buying is well suited is the specialist. If you focus on a narrow field, such as Kentucky rifles, French porcelain, or Art Nouveau jewelry, you will seldom find enough locally to satisfy your needs, wherever you are situated. The great advantage of buying by mail is that the whole country and, at least in theory, the whole world become a source of supply.

But, of course, as with everything else, there are a few disadvantages. The major one in this field is that you never quite know what you are buying, and disputes as to seller representations, quality, and the like may prove difficult to resolve in your favor. Whether you are buying out of a house, at auction, or from another local dealer, you always have or should have an opportunity to examine fully an object prior to purchasing it. This is seldom the case in mail order, where you must make your decision on the basis of a description or, at best, a photograph.

Locating Mail-Order Sources

Trade publications, such as *Art and Antiques, Antique Review,* and *Collector,* contain many dealer advertisements. For thousands of ads from both dealers and nondealers, try the *Antique Trader Weekly.* This extraordinary tabloid is hard on the eyes—most of the notices are about one by two inches and in tiny type—but it can be a gold mine. One of the nation's most important private collections of woven coverlets was largely built through advertisements in the *Trader.*

In selecting advertisers to approach, always give preference to those located nearest you. Problems can often be resolved more readily where the seller is located within your state or within a few hours' drive. It also means the possibility of a short buying trip rather than a transcontinental mail purchase. But, of course, the grass is always greener in far pastures; and chances are that what you want will be available only from distant suppliers. In selecting these, information as to the advertiser's knowledge and reputation is always valuable. If colleagues have been buying from certain advertisers, they may tell you something about them. Then again, they probably won't—especially if they have been buying well. Sharing sources is not a high priority with most dealers!

However, there are other ways to assess an advertiser. Is her or she a member of an antiques dealers association? Is the advertisement well written and indicative of knowledge of the objects being offered? Does it feature a picture and, if so, is it of good quality?

There are those, of course, who love to seek out people who don't know their merchandise, thinking thereby to get a bargain, but it is particularly important in mail-order buying that buyer and seller understand each other. In most cases, you will do the best buying from knowledgeable sources.

Remember, you need not simply select from what is offered. You can run your own notice listing the categories of antiques and collectibles you are seeking. Such "want lists" should be fairly specific and should spell out any particular limits on your purchases—for example, you may want nothing with restoration or no toys made after 1930. If you are looking for something fairly esoteric, such as a particular type of patented apple peeler or nutmeg grater, you might even want to run a picture of the item so that potential sellers will know exactly what you are after. And a phrase, such as "Clip and Save" or "Continually Seeking," will let people know that you are a constant customer for this sort of merchandise.

The effectiveness of want ads is often directly related to where they are placed. You don't run a request for Native American pottery and beadwork in a doll magazine or one for dolls in the publication of the Early American Industries Association. Target your audience, and you will save both time and money. Ads for specialized needs should be placed in specialized publications, and ads for general antiques and collectibles should be placed in broad-spectrum tabloids.

Answering an Advertisement

Ours is a fast-moving society. Gone are the days when you could respond to a notice in a trade paper by a letter, even with a check enclosed. If you see something you like, get on the telephone as quickly as possible. Chances are that a half-dozen other readers are interested in the same item or items. In fact, if you buy extensively by mail order you may decide to have key trade publications mailed to you first class. It costs a lot more, but if you are located in Florida or Oregon it is the only hope you have of competing with eastern buyers for items advertised in eastern publications.

Once you have reached the advertiser, be prepared with specific queries about what you are interested in. Size, age, condition, and details of provenance are all highly relevant. Remember, even if you have seen a picture of the piece, this does not tell all. Learn as much as you can. In the long run it will be best for both you and the seller.

Assume, for example, that you have answered an ad for an "Amish quilt." There is much you need to ask. Where is the quilt from? (Pennsylvania Amish quilts in general bring higher prices than those from Ohio or Indiana); what are the colors and fabrics? (wools and blues and blacks indicate earlier, more valuable examples; acrylics mean reproductions); is it signed or dated? (a big plus even if the date is from the 1930s); what is the condition? (must be described in detail: staining, wear, tears, etc.; these are critical to quilt value and seldom show in a photograph); how large is it? (very large quilts and those with corners cut for an old four-poster bed can be hard to sell); and, of course, what is the dealer price?

Ideally, the advertiser should have the piece in front of him or her when fielding these questions (that would be the case if you were in the shop), and you should make note of the responses so that you may compare them later with the quilt if you choose to buy it. If satisfied on all of the above, you should then inquire about the dealer's return policy. No reputable mail-order advertiser sells "as is." There should always be some reasonable provision for return if the piece does not measure up to its description. In fact, lack of such provision would make one suspect that this was a not a dealer to do business with.

Payment is the next question. For their own protection, advertisers usually require that payment be made by money order, certified check, credit card (when possible), or by personal check with the understanding that the goods will be held until the funds have cleared. Obviously, this puts the buyer at a disadvantage in the event that the merchandise is not shipped, is lost, or a dispute later arises regarding its quality. However, that is the way of the trade.

The best protection for the buyer is the series of questions outlined above and a written receipt or invoice setting forth a description of the piece consistent with the seller's answers to those. With this in hand, you should be in a pretty good position should there be any dispute later. Over the years, I have found that if one is careful, the number of problems in buying mail order is minimal. Most people are both honest and concerned to provide exact descriptions and provenance.

Shipping

Once a decision has been made and form of payment agreed upon, the next step is to arrange for packing and shipping. If you are dealing with someone who does a lot of mail-order business, he or she probably already has the system down.

Nevertheless, you should make your own opinion known.

Shipment should be in heavy cardboard packing cases, preferably double-packed (a smaller box within a larger one), with items individually wrapped and all surrounded with bubble pack or Styrofoam "popcorn." Shippers tend to try to get everything into one box, because it saves time and money, but *you* will be paying for shipping (that, too, is the rule), so you should insist that things not be crowded.

Shipment should be by an interstate carrier, preferably United Parcel Service, which, I have found, gets things there quickly and safely and also honors damage claims with a minimum of red tape. An excellent alternative, if you and the seller are located near communities with stops, is the package service of the Greyhound or Trailways bus line. This is often the fastest method of delivery and, again, a sure one. I do not recommend the United States Postal Service. There are too many stories of lost or damaged packages; insurance claims are handled slowly and with a low degree of cooperation.

Whatever the method of shipment, you should agree with the seller on insurance coverage, normally at your expense. You, as the buyer, should be the named insured, and coverage should be for the full cost. One may insure for the retail value of an item, thereby factoring in potential profit, but if a claim is made, few carriers will pay more than the cost figure.

What to Do if Something
Goes Wrong

The down side of the mail-order business involves several possible problems. First, there is the question of outright fraud. You answer an ad, send a check, and nothing arrives. Telephone calls go unanswered, letters are refused, and it becomes evident that the putative seller will give you neither goods nor a refund. What to do?

The short answer is: not much. If the transaction is across state lines, a question of mail fraud is involved. However, it is clear that the federal government and the postal authorities, burdened with what they view as more serious offenses, will take action only if a series or pattern of such incidents can be shown. A single transgression is not enough to warrant their intervention. Moreover, the people who run fraudulent ads are often hard to find and, when found, usually have nothing against which to levy a claim. Within the state one can either bring the matter to the attention of the attorney general or other appropriate authority or consider a civil suit (which is almost always prohibitively expensive considering the cost of legal services relative to the value of the item in question).

All this would be particularly discouraging to the would-be mail-order customer except for the fact that advertisers rarely behave in this manner. Fraud is simply not a major problem in the field.

What can be a problem, though, is misunderstanding due to different views of age of a particular item, condition, country of origin, and the like. No matter how carefully the buyer questions and how responsibly the seller answers, there will be times when what you get is not what you thought you ordered. This is why a clear understanding on the dealer's return policy is important. If this exists, preferably in writing, one should simply be able to point out the discrepancies and return the item for a refund.

Any responsible seller is more concerned with his or her reputation than with any single sale, and will, consequently, accept the return of antiques or collectibles (in the same condition they were shipped, of course) on any reasonable ground. But your responsibility as buyer is both to document your objections and to make them within a reasonable time (certainly, within ten days of delivery).

A final concern is with insurance claims. If something is damaged in shipment it is normally the buyer's responsibility to file the claim, and he or she must look to the shipper rather than the seller for compensation. In order to support your claim, you should preserve all of the damaged item: the carton and packing in which it came and any invoice, bill, canceled check, or other documentation of the transaction. Both common carriers and the United States Postal Service have very clear procedures that must be followed in damage claims, and one of the most important is timeliness. Don't dally about filing a claim: notification within twenty-four hours is preferable.

All in all, problems in the mail-order business are relatively few compared with the advantages of being able to buy at a distance and to select from a variety of items unavailable in any one location.

10.

FAKES

Though collectors and legitimate dealers never regard it as such, the proliferation of fakes and reproductions in the antiques and collectibles world is really a compliment to the trade. Collecting has come of age. The objects being bought and sold are now of sufficient value to warrant the effort and investment involved in the production of first-class fakes!

This is not to say, of course, that faking is something new. Roman collectors complained of false Grecian statues, and the Chinese were reproducing Sung dynasty bronzes within a few hundred years of their origin. Closer to our own time, prestigious museums such as the Williamsburg and the Metropolitan Museum of Art have had to tuck away pieces once thought to be of the eighteenth century but now known to have been manufactured in the 1920s and '30s. Yet evidence indicates that the making of reproductions and outright fakes is more widespread today than it has ever been. Why so?

There are two obvious reasons for this increase in chicanery. On the one hand, the variety of collectible objects is far greater than it has been ever before, and many of these objects combine the appeal of being both expensive and easy to reproduce. Very few people have the skills to even passably imitate a Renoir or a Rembrandt, but it isn't difficult to fake the grain paint on a nineteenth-century pine table or to put together a "Shaker" cupboard from hundred-year-old boards. Either of the latter might bring a minimum of one thousand to five thousand dollars at auction, while the outlay in materials is minimal.

Moreover, advances in technology have aided the faker far more than the potential victim. The development of high-impact extruded plastics that look and feel just like bone has made the area of scrimshaw a veritable mine field for collectors, while recently developed paints make convincing alterations (such as the addition of a signature or an American flag to a ship's mast) that greatly increase the salability of an ordinary nineteenth-century painting. What is there to do?

Avoiding Getting "Stuck"

The three keys to not buying fakes are knowledge, source, and circumstance. The first, knowledge, is rather obvious. If you have cultivated a sophisticated taste in a given area, be it pressed glass or pre-Columbian pottery (both of which, incidentally, are real rats' nests of falsity), you will probably be hard to fool. If you know how things are made, when they were made, by whom and the characteristics of his or her crafts-manship, the indicia of their age, and the approximate number of legitimate examples currently in the market, you make it difficult for someone to take you for a ride.

Of course, the problem is that most of us cannot hope to reach this level of knowledge in more than one or two fields, even if that. Yet we usually buy and sell a variety of things, many of which we know only superficially. It is easy to say, "learn"; but few have the time or inclination to develop a more encompassing expertise.

We must rely, then, on source and circumstance. The former, while never infallible, can be a very good guide. It is not without reason that a knowledgeable buyer will always ask, "Where did you get this?" If you buy from reputable dealers or auction houses you greatly reduce your chances of getting burned. This is not because such sources are immune to error (they certainly aren't!) or because they only employ honest personnel (they don't always) but because anyone who has established a reputation in the business knows how easily it might be destroyed by even a hint of impropriety. People at this level try to avoid questionable merchandise, and if a problem develops with something they have sold, they will almost always take it back without question. They understand very well that reputation is far more important than any single sale. Any of these sources should always provide a written bill of sale describing your purchase in full, just as it was represented to you. Unwillingness to furnish such a document (which can be the basis for an action for breach of contract or warranty) is an immediate warning signal.

Dealing with people you do not know and about whom you can learn very little obviously has definite risks. This is especially true if the individual or individuals seem to have no known address or fixed place of abode—a situation surprisingly common with truckers and pickers. If you enter into a transaction with such a character and the piece involved later proves to be "wrong," you will probably have trouble finding him or her, much less recovering your money.

The final element, circumstance, is best illustrated by one of the most famous frauds of our time. A few years ago, a seemingly extraordinary seventeenth-century armchair appeared on the New England market, eventually wending its way to a prestigious American museum (which shall remain

nameless here, as its staff has already been subjected to sufficient ridicule). Bought from an "important" dealer for a five-
figure sum, the chair was proudly displayed, only to be exposed
by the man who had "baited the hook," a disgruntled but highly
skilled craftsman who had created the chair in order, as he saw
it, to show up stuffed-shirt, elitist museum people.

The museum, of course, initially denied that the piece was
a fake. However, the maker pointed out that he was in possession of certain missing parts of the chair that experts
assumed had been lost in the nineteenth century, and,
most tellingly, he pointed out that the holes for stretchers
in the chair had been made with an electric drill, something
hardly available during the 1600s! A simple X ray of the frame
would have disclosed this discrepancy, but none was made.
Why?

The "why" is really what circumstance is all about. This
chair was of a type so rare that the last comparable example had
been uncovered in the 1920s. Yet it showed up in plain view
on the porch of a Maine house (where it had, of course, been
planted). Moreover, while the first dealer or two who handled
it may have lacked the knowledge to evaluate the chair fully,
it soon came into the hands of people sophisticated enough to
analyze it thoroughly. That they did not do so reflects a common failing among all of us. They did not look closely at the
chair because they did not want to look closely! It was not only
a question of the money to be made on each transaction as the
piece marched ever upward toward its destined niche in the
museum world; it was also the prestige involved. Each individual was now in the position of being able to say that he or she
had taken part in the discovery of a great American rarity. Why,
then, look too closely? Why rock the boat?

But looking closely is what must be done. Whenever you
are offered what seems to be a great rarity or a piece that is
priced far below comparable examples, you should imme-

diately become concerned. This does not mean that you should turn your back on an opportunity to buy just because it seems too good to be true. It does mean, though, that you should proceed with caution, bringing in an expert in the field or supplementing your own judgment by some other means.

Sometimes the most obvious clues are ignored. Just recently, numerous forged examples of "Texana" (a term used for historical documents relating to the state of Texas) were uncovered by an expert, who pointed out that not only were the examples in question rather poor copies but the number of them offered on the market in the last several years exceeded by five or ten times the number of known legitimate examples that had appeared in the past century! Yet nobody found this odd.

Inquiry is the key. Don't be afraid to ask about something you are buying, and then evaluate what you have learned: who owned the piece, how long it has been known locally, when and where the last similar example surfaced, is it of a type known to be faked? Questions like these may not reveal a fake, but, if properly answered, they should make you (and your eventual customer) feel a lot better about the origin of the piece. And, most important, don't ever let your natural greed for fame or fortune blind you to the reality of the unlikelihood of your discovery.

Problematic Areas

Entire books have been devoted to the study of fakes (a good recent example is John Bly's *Is It Genuine?*), and little would be accomplished by a superficial examination of the field. However, certain general guidelines may be helpful.

Objects faked today usually fall into one of two categories:

items that are easily reproduced because they are cast in molds or because their fabrication does not require great technical skill, and items that sell for such high prices that the time, effort, and expense necessary to create them is justified by the potential profit.

In the first category may be placed such molded or cast items as pressed glass, weathervanes, cast-iron toys and banks, and various forms of pottery and porcelain. All these are being churned out in quantity either from master molds that have survived over the years or molds made from a legitimate example. In many cases, the reproductions are not originally designed to defraud and may even be marked with the name of a twentieth-century manufacturer (as with the historical bottles made at New Jersey's Clevenger Glass Works and the numerous pieces of scrimshaw turned out by various seafaring museums). However, unscrupulous individuals may file off company ciphers, apply false signs of wear, and attempt to pass the pieces off as period.

One of the better ways to keep track of these often crude attempts is to frequent gift and crafts shops as well as suppliers of reproductions. The latter advertise to the trade in most antiques publications.

Fakes do not have to be cast to be inexpensive. For decades, this country has been flooded with thousands of false pieces of "pre-Columbian" art. Sun- or kiln-dried and hand-painted in Mexico and Central America, these imposters probably comprise ninety percent of all such artifacts on the market. Since the end of World War II they have been joined by a seemingly endless supply of African art. In both cases, the natural artistry of an indigenous people is combined with a low pay scale to create often charming pieces that, unfortunately, are seldom what they are represented to be.

As one might imagine, the more costly items are, the less common they are. Furniture has long been preeminent here.

As far back as the 1870s, extremely fine reproductions of eighteenth-century American furniture were on the market, and in England and France the copying of period styles developed at an even earlier date. The best are made exactly as were the originals, and such exactitude is not without its price. It may easily cost fifteen thousand dollars or more to fake an eighteenth-century mahogany highboy or secretary. But, of course, the piece may be sold for five times that much, offering the seller substantial motivation for the deed. The greatest protection most of us have against such fraud is that we will never have the money to buy such a creation!

Bear in mind, too, that legitimate (circa 1880–1920) furniture reproductions in the so-called Colonial Revival style are now considered highly collectible and may bring as much as five thousand dollars for a large case piece. As long as these are properly represented they should be welcomed to the market as a happy, affordable substitute for the pricey originals.

Remedies for Misrepresentation

Your recourse if you are sold a fake will depend largely on how careful you were about identifying your seller and insisting on a written warranty as to period and provenance. If you did the right things here, you will probably get your money back rather easily; on the other hand, sellers who give you the right name, address, and description of merchandise sold are also least likely to slip you a bad item! It's the others you have to worry about.

Lawsuits between dealers and between dealers and collectors over these issues are a lot more common than one might imagine, and not all are resolved in favor of the aggrieved party. If you do not have an "airtight" case against the seller, it may not be worthwhile to proceed, especially in light of the legal fees involved. Everyone gets skinned once in a while.

Your best defenses against fraud are knowledge and dispassionate analysis. Your worst enemy is greed. Thinking you are about to make a killing in the market is often the first step toward getting killed!

II.

SELLING

The ability to sell your antiques and collectibles, whether to other dealers or to the public, through shows, auction, mail order, or from your home or shop is the key to success in the field. This may seem quite obvious; after all, in every retail and wholesale business the object is to sell the merchandise, not hoard it or part with it grudgingly. But there are many in the antiques world who regard selling as a necessary evil rather than an end in itself.

Most dealers are collectors first and often have gone into business to upgrade their own collections. For them the hunt and the acquisition are the main thing. They sell so as to have money to buy! This is really an appealing idea, certainly more so than the greed that seems to motivate so much of business; but it is often in conflict with the realities of the field.

If you buy only what you like, refuse to learn to recognize bargains in other areas, and won't sell the best you find because you want to keep it for your own collection, you will be operating under severe handicaps. Successful sellers of antiques and collectibles are good businesspeople. They know how to sell, and they avoid becoming too attached to those things which pass through their hands.

Wholesale or Retail?

The best, most efficient dealers are usually those who enjoy their work. Choose the field where you feel most comfortable. If you are really a "picker" at heart, much more interested in the great find and the wheeling and dealing of the auction market than in personal contacts with retail customers, wholesale may be the place for you.

Dealers speak a special language and share a certain type of camaraderie that is, perhaps, unique to the field. Few hope to get rich at what they do. Their wealth is in stored-up experiences; memories of treasures found and lost; tales of fabulous auctions, sales, and shows. When you sell to a knowledgeable dealer you share not only a financial transaction but also an intellectual exchange replete with arcane language, gamesmanship, and shared adventures.

The retail customer, unless a long-time and knowledgeable collector, is quite another matter. Most must be "sold"; that is, urged, cajoled, and encouraged to purchase something they usually know relatively little about. Much information regarding an item's condition, provenance, and historical background, which need not even be discussed with a fellow dealer (who already knows), must be gone over carefully both to encourage the buyer's confidence and to provide him or her with sufficient background to make an intelligent choice.

Not everyone enjoys making sales "pitches." You may prefer dealing with fellow experts who walk into your shop or booth, turn a few things over, and say, "Okay, I'll take that and that and that, what's your best price?" If this is true for you, you may enjoy the wholesale field.

Every dealer does a lot of wholesale business. Still, a total commitment to wholesale is a different matter. Many come to it because they don't enjoy the pressures and politics of the show circuit or can't stand sitting around in a shop. Wholesale allows time to be on the road. You operate by appointment, in most cases dealing with a relatively small number of dealer-customers who visit you (or whom you visit) once or twice a month.

On the other hand, if you like socializing and meeting people of other backgrounds, you can do very well in retail. Some of the most financially successful dealers don't even have an in-depth knowledge of their stock, but they have the ability to sell. They like their customers, and they convey a feeling of trust. Of course, you want to be a knowledgeable dealer, whatever your field. Whether you choose wholesale or retail, knowledge and an understanding of the client's needs are the keys to success.

Establishing a Clientele

In both wholesale and retail—but especially in the latter (after all, most dealers would buy from Attila the Hun if he had good, cheap "merch"!)—the key to long-range financial stability is to establish a dependable clientele. To do so you must not only sell desirable objects at fair prices but also create enduring relationships with customers.

Particularly in the retail trade, reputation is extremely important. Some dealers come to the business with a built-in advantage in this regard. The higher financial levels of the antiques world tend to be very social, and wealth, the right family name, or corporate connections can open doors forever closed to others far more knowledgeable. However, reputation can also be earned. The dealer who, over a period of years, sells good merchandise at reasonable prices and deals fairly with his or her clients will develop a following. Integrity is extremely important. Many customers who come to you either have had unfortunate experiences with other dealers or are aware, through the media, of various scandals that have rocked the trade and the auction world over the past few years. They have a right to be suspicious. Your responsibility is to show them that you are different. A few basic policies should suffice.

Always disclose everything you know about a piece, good or bad. If there are repairs not obvious to the untrained eye, point them out, noting that the price reflects these imperfections. Be willing to provide a written bill of sale setting forth everything you have stated to the customer regarding the period or condition of an object. *If you don't want to put it in writing, don't say anything about period or condition!* If the customer asks a question about a piece under consideration and you don't know the answer, say you will try to obtain the information—and do so. Don't bluff. People don't expect you to know everything, but they do expect you to tell the truth.

View every transaction as part of an ongoing relationship. Anyone who comes into your shop or booth, particularly if he or she buys, should become part of a customer list containing name, address, and, where pertinent, collecting interests. Few dealers seem willing to take the time to do this sort of thing, yet with the advent of computers, maintaining and revising such a file has become quite easy.

A customer list can be used in several ways. If you have openings or special exhibits, you can generate invitations. Notes can be sent to collectors whenever you acquire an item of interest to them (knowing that you have purchasers for particular pieces may allow you to pay more for them than you would were you buying on "spec"). If you are selling by mail order, a customer list is usually far superior to blind advertising in targeting potential purchasers.

When problems arise (as they will), be flexible and take the long view. Suppose you sell a quilt to someone who comes back a month later saying that it doesn't match the bedroom wallpaper. Many dealers would say "tough luck." That is seldom a fruitful approach. Sure, you could keep the money, but you'd probably lose the customer—not to mention everyone else whom he or she chooses to tell about your "outrageous" behavior.

Your reputation is, in the long run, your most important asset. No one sale is important enough to jeopardize that. As a general rule, I feel that anything returned within a reasonable time (some dealers' billheads list a period, usually thirty days) and in good condition should be accepted, no matter what the excuse offered. Certainly, a refund should be given when a customer claims that the piece is not as you represented it, even though you have little doubt that the item is "right." Arguing accomplishes little. On the other hand, you should make it clear that the refund is being given as a matter of policy, and that as far as you are concerned the object is just as you described it. "But," you may say, "other retail businesses don't usually have such flexible return policies. People will take advantage of me." It may be true that other retailers take a different view of returns, but in a certain way the antiques and collectibles field is not like other fields. It is a uniquely personal area where people generally expect and receive special consideration. If you don't feel comfortable with this, be a wholesaler. Dealers are assumed to buy on their own judgment, and barring outright misrepresentation, professionals don't return things. As to customers taking undue advantage, it seldom happens. In fact, returns seem to be far lower than in other retail fields such as clothing and home appliances.

Helping People to Upgrade

Though you may start out modestly enough, perhaps selling inexpensive items such as Depression glass or fifties memorabilia, if you are like most dealers you will have higher aspirations. Indeed, you may dream of trading in Meissen porcelain,

Sung dynasty bronzes, or Oriental carpets. If so, take your clients with you.

Major dealers of long standing can boast of customer relationships extending back decades. In many cases, these customers started out buying rather ordinary things, in keeping with both their taste at the time and their economic situation. However, as time passed and they prospered, they followed their dealer's advice and moved into new and more sophisticated areas. He or she, in turn, supported by this patronage, was able to handle more costly items.

Always encourage your clients to upgrade their collections, and be prepared to sell to their developing taste. Otherwise, they will go elsewhere. Moreover, show a willingness to take back in trade items the clients have lost interest in. In most cases, these will have increased in value, so that you will profit by the arrangement, but whatever the situation, your clients should be able to use the pieces as a form of down payment on better-grade antiques or collectibles that you sell them. You will be helping each other and you will maintain the relationship.

Other things being equal, such as taste, sources of merchandise, and financial backing, it is the dealer who takes the long view who not only survives but prospers as well. Whether you sell at shows, from home or shop, or through the mail, you will always do best if you have a firm customer base. The person who looks at business as unconnected, single sales seldom does well or lasts long.

12.

SELLING FROM A SHOP

*T*here was a time when the term "shop" was synonymous with the antiques trade. Dealers always had their own spaces, often cramped and cluttered but filled with a variety of wonderful objects. The proprietors, whether located in New York or in Boston or along some New England or midwestern byway, were usually characters whose idiosyncrasies often became as well-known as their merchandise.

Things have changed greatly, though, over the past twenty or thirty years. The vast increase in the number of collectors, the emphasis on auction with its lure of high prices and sudden notoriety, and, most of all, accelerating costs have made business more difficult for the individual shopkeeper.

Novice collectors, who expect to buy antiques the same way they acquire home furnishings, groceries, or electronics, are not willing to seek out the isolated, individual dealer. Auctioneers with their instant cash have cut sharply into the dealers' sources of supply. And landlords, eager to cater to fast-food outlets and boutiques, have pushed rents to a point where dealers can no longer afford to operate in the areas where their best customers are found—large cities and affluent suburbs. As a consequence, anyone who wishes to run his or her own shop should proceed carefully, for the independence and satisfaction of having one's own "place" must be balanced against the financial burdens it brings.

Choosing a Space

Your first consideration in selecting a shop must be whether or not the business really requires one, and, if so, what type. If you wish to run a general antiques emporium with an emphasis on walk-in trade and spontaneous sales (particularly of low-end items), a shop is the best way to go. In fact, you may want a spot with a big front window on the busiest street in town. But if you are a specialist selling items of limited appeal to the general public, it is quite possible that you do not need a store. If you do want a store, you can do quite nicely with an upstairs, out-of-the-way location.

Location, then, is a key factor. As a general rule it is best to be situated where there are other dealers, decorators, crafts shops, and similar operations, because they draw receptive crowds. Antiques and collectibles businesses differ from most retail operations in that they actually thrive on competition. The more stores in a given area, the more customers there are. Moreover, most dealers are glad to suggest the name of a neighbor who might have something they don't. Can you imagine a car dealership doing that?

Many cities and small towns have antiques areas where dealers are clustered. Rents may be higher here, but the extra expense will often be justified by the greater business potential. Whatever the location you are considering, you should first visit some neighboring merchants. Inquire about business (in general terms, of course; if you try to interrogate people you'll rarely get answers), street traffic, security, and neighborhood reputation. These last two factors can be very important. If burglary is a common occurrence in the area, you will want to go elsewhere or allocate extra money for security. If the locality is considered "in" for shoppers, you can probably count on drawing the right kind of street traffic. If, on the other hand, people are pestered by vagrants or feel unsafe after dark, even the lowest rental will usually not justify locating there. Remember, once you sign a lease, it can be difficult to get out of it. You want to be sure that you are making the right choice.

Equally important is the question of cost. You should not enter into a store lease without having consulted an attorney and, perhaps, your accountant. It is not possible to do more than generalize about such things, but as a rule you should not lease a space without having on hand the money to cover a year's rental plus whatever security (usually one or two months) is required. Dealers who go into business thinking they will pay their rent from each month's profits are dealers who fail.

The first year or two is always hard; that is why the IRS will let you operate at a loss for two years without showing undue concern. Rent, utilities, advertising, and the replacement—almost always at higher cost—of merchandise sold are all factors to be considered. If you lack the capital to survive, you are far better off doing shows or selling from your home or by mail order.

Another factor to be considered is timing. Try to avoid going into business during a slow period: August in New York City or Florida, or February in New England. It may be easier to get space at that time, but the lack of patronage will put you at an immediate disadvantage. Ideally, you will open your shop at the height of the local season. There will be more customers, more activity, and a greater chance for publicity.

Designing a Shop Space

Unless previously used as an antiques or collectibles shop, few stores serve this purpose without at least some modification.

How much alteration your space will require depends in part upon the nature of your business.

If you plan to sell furniture or other large objects, you will need wide doors, if possible a loading ramp and parking area for large vehicles, and a substantial adjacent storage area. You should not be in a position where you must have everything on the floor at one time, much less have the plight of some city dealers, who actually have to put furniture on the street in all sorts of weather just so they and their customers can get into the shop!

If you plan to do restoration, refinishing, chair seating, or furniture stripping, you should also have a well-ventilated, fire-resistant area for these tasks. As discussed elsewhere, insurance on antiques and collectibles is both costly and, in some cases, hard to obtain. You want to minimize the possibility of accidents.

The ideal interior is generally a single open space, the size of which will vary depending on your needs. If you sell jewelry, you can get by quite nicely with a fifteen-by-eighteen-foot area. Almost anything else requires more room. Clusters of small rooms and halls should be avoided, because they make display difficult, as well as posing security problems.

If you anticipate and seek substantial walk-in trade, you should have a window; it will often prove your best advertisement.

The question of a sign (size, location, materials) should be investigated before you choose a site. Most communities regulate shop signs, and you need to know what you can and can't do in a given location. This issue can be especially critical in rural areas, where shops are often located off the main road, thus requiring directional signs. In many areas, in the name of "beautification," the size and form of these signs are either strictly regulated, or signs may be forbidden altogether.

How you design the shop interior is a matter of personal preference, though the trend today is toward a single open space with a minimum of wall shelving. This allows more flexibility in the arrangement of merchandise. Smaller things can be placed on top of furniture or, if more valuable, in locked cases.

White walls and track lighting are the popular choice. They both highlight the merchandise and avoid the distractions of "busy" wallpaper and oddly located wall and ceiling lights. In addition, the painting and the installation of the lighting system, being relatively simple, can often be done by the shopkeeper, thus keeping expenses down. Floors should be polyurethaned wood or tile, especially if furniture is to be moved about on them. Unless displayed for sale, avoid rugs. They can cause accidents, are easily damaged, and gather dust.

An alternate form of decoration is the "rustic" look, featuring walls covered with barn siding or shingles. While sometimes distracting, this decor creates a sort of nostalgia in certain customers that may be very conducive to sales. The same may be said of theme decoration. For example, if you feature country-store items—tins, old bottles, advertising signs, and the like—you might decide to set your interior up in the form of a country store.

Ultimately, the store should reflect a combination of your approach to your merchandise and an awareness (gained by observing other shops and talking to their owners) of what seems to appeal to the local clientele.

Display

The basic problem every antiques and collectibles shop owner faces is "the quest for the new." When you open a shop you can anticipate a rush of customers. (If you don't get that traffic you have picked either the wrong place or the wrong time.) Dealers will hurry in to see if you have anything that is underpriced.

Collectors and browsers will want to see what's new in town.

After their initial trips, they will be back, but only once or twice unless you can show them some fresh merchandise. To maintain return trade you must create the impression that your inventory is exciting and well priced *and* constantly being renewed. One solution, of course, is just to keep buying. Unfortunately, this is not practical for most shopkeepers. Not only are good antiques and collectibles both costly and hard to find, there is only so much space in a shop. Something must be sold in order for a new item to take its place.

There are ways, however, to create an impression of freshness with a minimal amount of actual inventory change. The easiest solution is to keep moving things around. Change your window or chief display areas every week. Windows, particularly, should mirror seasonal themes: Christmas, Spring, Thanksgiving, and the like. Though we all look, we do not always "see." It is an interesting phenomenon, experienced by every dealer: a customer will come in and fall in love with the same piece he or she passed by a week ago. Last week it was in a different place and either unseen or unappreciated in that context.

Further, it is best not to show everything in stock at the same moment. Hold back perhaps ten to fifteen percent so that these items can be judiciously added to your wares over a period of time, thus creating an impression of newness. By the same token, if something has been on the shelves for several weeks and has not sold, put it away. Let it rest for a few months, then bring it out in an entirely new context. For example, a doll that has appeared with other dolls or in a cradle might emerge as part of an advertising collectibles display.

It is not always easy to follow these rules, as most of us feel that the more we have on the floor, the more choices customers have and the more likely they are to buy. Yet things often do not work that way. Potential buyers may be overwhelmed by "too much"; and it is important to make them feel that these things are rare and hard to come by. Satiation does *not* whet the appetite.

Labeling is also important. Most of your customers will know relatively little about what you are selling, and many will be reluctant to ask. A small card containing historical information (as well as the price) should be attached to each piece in the shop. Such tidbits often promote a sale where otherwise there would not be one ("This is a rocker of the type favored by President Kennedy," for example). People like to feel they know something about their purchases, and many will be impressed by your knowledge.

In the same vein, if you find that an object you have for sale is similar to one illustrated in a book on antiques or collectibles, place the book, open to the appropriate page, next to your example. This gives it an aura of authenticity for most collectors.

Wherever possible, link your merchandise, your shop, and yourself to national and local events, historical or contemporary: for example, a painting of George Washington for Washington's birthday, or Elvis memorabilia for *his* birthday. This provides a feeling of timeliness, the "now" syndrome that everyone from boutique to auto-dealership owners uses to create in customers a sense of urgency to buy. Auctioneers have been exceedingly clever in achieving this feeling of immediacy, but few dealers have followed suit.

Security

Shop security is always of prime importance. Your initial concern must be with exterior entrances. Before you bought or rented your space you should have inquired of the police department and neighbors as to the frequency of burglary and robbery in the area. Too high a rate would suggest that you should look elsewhere.

Secondly, you should examine approaches to the building and the exterior lighting. Back and side doors, dark alleyways, and windows that open onto unguarded lots are all potential problems. Are there enough street lights in the area? If not, you may have to install exterior lights, particularly behind the building. In any case, you will always want to keep lights on in the shop, both for reasons of security and because illuminated window displays are an effective form of advertising.

All doors should be reinforced with sheet steel or heavy plywood and have pick-proof dead-bolt or mortise locks. Windows and skylights should be barred or equipped with accordion gates with padlocks. However, before installing these, check with local authorities, because they are sometimes forbidden by fire codes as hindering escape during a blaze.

Though expensive, alarm systems can be very effective, particularly if hooked up to the local police station. Turning them on and off may seem complicated at first, but even the least mechanically minded soon can manage. The biggest problem is being awakened in the middle of the night because a short circuit or other electrical disturbance has activated the system.

Perhaps the best alarm system is the neighborhood. If you and your neighbors keep an eye on one another's property, it will go a long way toward reducing theft. When you are doing a show or going off on a buying trip, let a neighbor know. Then, if he (or she) sees a truck in front of your place in the wee hours, he will call the police. You, of course, will do the same for him. This sort of neighborhood watch makes an area unhealthy for criminals.

In-store security is another matter, but, again, it is a question of prevention. You don't want to be in the position of having to confront someone who has just stolen from you. He or she may be dangerous—or, if you are wrong in your suspicions, you may face a suit for false arrest. What you want to do is to make it so hard to pilfer that thieves will go elsewhere.

Store layout is a factor here. There should be a single entrance, and your desk or work area should be adjacent to it. Small, valuable things should be kept in locked cases and removed only by you (for a fuller discussion of this matter see chapter 13, "Selling on the Show Circuit"). Uncased, smaller objects should not be placed near exits, and the room should be designed so that you have good sight lines to all areas.

On the other hand, such things as overhead mirrors, and signs stating that shoplifters will be prosecuted, or the like are inappropriate—and so is the practice of following one's customers about the shop. Any respectable client will not tolerate this sort of thing and will not return. After all, this is a genteel business, not a supermarket!

Bad checks are another problem. Today, no one can operate on a cash-only basis. Credit cards are mandatory for any major business. The cost of the system simply must be built into prices. However, you will still need to accept checks, and some of them will bounce.

It is not easy to protect yourself from the professional con man (or woman). He or she will have all the identification (all false, of course) anyone could ask for. It is the legitimate customer who can produce only an old library card! Nevertheless, you should ask for identification and a home telephone number.

If the sale is a major one running into the thousands of dollars, you should try to reach either the telephone number given or a bank reference before releasing the merchandise. Admittedly, this is an imperfect system—it might not be banking hours and there may well be no one home—but it's the only system we have. If you do not get results from your inquiries, you should insist on holding the purchases until the check has cleared.

Be assured that you will lose some sales this way. You will offend honest buyers, and they will probably not return. Still, the incidence of bad-check passing has become so high throughout the nation that you must protect yourself.

Antiques Centers

One of the answers to the problems involved in running a shop—attracting customers, carrying high overhead, and providing security—has been the antiques center. First appearing on the West Coast a decade or more ago, these multidealer complexes have spread throughout the country.

The first were cooperatives with several dealers banding together to share costs, floor time, and decisions on such things as advertising and who sweeps the floor. Many people soon realized, though, that democratic as it was, cooperative decision-making was time-consuming and friction-provoking. Moreover, a group shop needed management, and most dealers wanted to sell, not manage.

The natural next step was the entry of the professional manager. Typically, he or she owns or rents the shop and leases booths or floor space to anywhere from a half-dozen to over a hundred dealers. Monthly rentals vary greatly. Some may be as little as fifty dollars, others may exceed three hundred dollars. The obligations of the parties involved (renters and managers alike) can be extensive.

Some managements guarantee a specific quantity of local and regional advertising under the contract cost. In other cases, dealers are required to share in the expense of such publicity. "Floor time," a period when the dealer will be present to sell not only from his or her booth but also from the booths of others, is sometimes required. In other instances, the management furnishes a professional staff. Under the latter system it is now not unusual to find an Ohio dealer simultaneously renting space in centers in New York, Maine, and Virginia. If he (or she) employs a trucker to carry new merchandise to his centers he may seldom, if ever, appear there. Everything is done by telephone and mail.

It is customary for the monthly rental charge to include the cost of utilities, such as light and heat. Telephone charges will be extra or management will furnish a pay phone. Generally, minimal cleaning of the booth areas is provided; sometimes management personnel will rearrange a booth after sales or on the arrival of new merchandise. Basically, top-notch management provides everything that a dealer would expect to have in his or her own shop.

Choosing a Center

There can be no doubt that antiques centers are the right business choice for many dealers. Costs are fixed by contract, the large number of other dealers should assure a good customer flow, and there is much more free time to look for fresh merchandise.

However, not all centers are successful, and not all successful centers are right for all dealers. You must choose carefully. A visit is almost mandatory, as is seeking the opinions of people who rent space and of those who shop in the center.

What is being sold? One of the most notable characteristics of the antiques center is that merchandise therein seeks the lowest level. If the manager is having trouble filling booths (usually because of slow sales rather than high rentals), he or she will be tempted to take in people selling reproductions, crafts, or new items. This, in turn, will lead to the rapid withdrawal of dealers with better-quality antiques and collectibles as well as the customers who sought them out. The center will become nothing but a flea market. See what the worst, not the best, dealers in the center sell. If you can live with that, it may be the place for you.

What is the emphasis of the center? Is it on country, on collectibles, or on glass and jewelry? Decide whether or not you fit into the scheme of things. If you do, you will probably sell. The next step is the details.

Examine the proposed contract carefully. Rent and floor time are, of course, important, but there are other things to consider. What is the management policy on theft and damage? In most cases, managers will take no responsibility for such losses. This is a major consideration, because daytime security in most centers is not very good. Typically, three or four people will staff a fifty-booth center, with most of them at the check-out counter or in their own booths (if there is a time-sharing arrangement). Losses are usually higher than in a small shop. You should feel free to ask about security arrangements, and you may decide not to put your better things in the center. You can also employ locked cases with the management holding the keys. That usually works well enough.

Another consideration is staff expertise. Unless they are themselves dealers (and often they aren't), management personnel may have only limited knowledge of what you are selling. They will lose sales because they don't know what something is, where it came from, or how it works, or because they lack authority to negotiate beyond the standard ten percent dealer's discount almost universal in centers.

If, having taken all these factors into consideration, you still feel that an antiques center is the right place for you to be, you can feel some security in knowing that this is probably the fastest-growing aspect of the antiques and collectibles field— the wave of the future.

Consignments

One way to stock any shop is through consignments. This involves taking in antiques and collectibles owned by others and selling them under your name (the public is not aware that they aren't yours) for an agreed-upon commission, usually twenty-five to thirty-three percent.

The obvious advantage of the consignment system is that you obtain merchandise without any capital investment. If it doesn't sell, you simply return it to the owner. There is no risk to you. Moreover, the rate of return compares favorably with the profit margin you could reasonably expect on most of your own purchases.

While some object to filling their premises with other people's merchandise, consignment is often a practical answer to the problem of limited acquisition funds. You can maintain that fresh look without spending a lot of money. However, to protect yourself and the consignor, you should follow some guidelines.

Every consignment should be made pursuant to a written agreement that

1. describes each consigned object clearly.

2. establishes the agreed-upon price and commission.

3. establishes the period of the consignment—usually ninety days is the maximum—at the end of which the consignor must pick up the piece. One of the problems with this system is getting people to take things away. After all, they didn't want them in the first place. That's why they brought them to you.

4. contains provision that the consignee will not be responsible for theft or damage, from whatever cause, occurring while the object is in his or her hands.

5. contains, if desired, a provision for the shopkeeper to lower the asking price on the piece if it does not sell. Usually the figures are ten percent after thirty days, twenty percent more after sixty days, back to the consignor after ninety days.

The biggest problem with consignment is that it is addictive. Once people start bringing you things and you start making commissions, it can be easy to fall further and further into the habit. But most of the offerings will not be of the quality you want, and accepting them may damage your reputation.

Don't allow this to happen. If a consignor says, "Well, if you won't take the old clothing and the used TV, you can't have the sterling sugar bowl," send him or her away. In order for the system to work for you, goods acquired on consignment must never amount to more than fifty percent of the stock on the floor, and you must have absolute control over what comes in. Don't make the consignor your partner!

Sale Days

I have a generally negative attitude about sales in antiques and collectibles shops. Most dealers are already giving discounts of one sort or another (dealer, decorator, and so on) to about half their clientele. Moreover, too many of the general public seem to feel that dealers acquire their goods either by finding them on the street or by tricking an elderly owner out of them. Offering sale prices is just further confirmation of the attitude that dealers are making too much on what they sell.

I recognize, though, that many in the trade swear by sales, especially as a way to clear out old merchandise. Still, if you are going to run a sale, it should be both a dignified procedure and limited in scope.

Keep your advertising minimal and not flamboyant. You are not disposing of year-old calendars or stale Easter candy. Sales should not be storewide clearances but should be focused on objects that have been in stock for too long or that you no longer wish to carry; and they should be conducted at slow times of the year, when they serve to draw in customers who might not otherwise visit you. A pre-Christmas sale, for example, is illogical. After all, this is the time that people should be doing the most buying. Save your sales for the quiet periods. Finally, don't have many sales; one or two in a year is quite enough. That way, people may look forward to them. If there are too many, they will mistake your shop for an outlet store!

13.

SELLING ON THE
SHOW CIRCUIT

Thirty years ago, there were but a few hundred antiques shows scattered across the United States. Today, they number in the thousands, reflecting not only the great increase in the number of collectors but also a developing preference on the part of dealers.

There are sound reasons for dealer interest in the show circuit. First, operating costs have risen steadily, making it more and more difficult to operate a shop, especially in larger cities and their suburbs; yet these are precisely the places where the majority of affluent collectors are to be found. The antiques and collectibles show offers a way to reach this audience more economically.

For the dealer new to the business, attracting a clientele is often the prime concern. Association with a show, especially one of good reputation and long standing in the community, ensures that the neophyte will have an audience.

Finally, selling at shows allows one to do more with less. If a shortfall in merchandise is your problem, the show circuit is one very effective answer. The same number of pieces, which would quickly become boring in a shop, can seem always fresh to a new audience. Just keep moving around and doing shows far enough apart that you get little customer overlap.

The Show Hierarchy

The world of antiques and collectibles shows is like a great pyramid. At the top are about a dozen major events, such as the Winter Antiques Show and the Fall or "Pier" Show, both in New York City; the High Museum Show in Atlanta; the Philadelphia Hospital Show; the Chicago International; the Theta Charity Show of Houston; and so forth. These represent perhaps one-tenth of one percent of all the antiques and collectibles events staged in this country and Canada during a year.

The "waist" of the pyramid, as it were, are hundreds of fine regional and local shows. Some of them are specialized (dolls, toys, folk art, Native American crafts, duck decoys, and weapons are popular categories), and many are linked to charitable organizations, churches, and other worthy causes.

Below this level, at the base of the pyramid, are thousands of one- or two-day antiques and collectibles expositions of varying quality and uncertain duration. Some have carried on for long periods. Others last a single year. Some may be a good place for the beginning dealer to gain experience. Few will justify a long relationship.

Choosing the Show for You

Before you decide if you want to "do" a particular antiques show, you should determine if you want to become involved in the show field at all. Talk to some dealers active on the circuit. See what they think about it. Being a show dealer often involves getting up in the wee hours, loading a van or truck with heavy objects, transporting them a considerable distance, unloading in semidarkness (rain and wind are other special treats), carrying things up stairs and through impossibly narrow hallways, setting up in a space much too small (or too big) for what you have brought, listening for eight hours to people tell you why they or their grandmother threw out things just like the ones you have, then packing up everything and taking it back home again . . . usually arriving just after midnight!

Don't let anyone tell you that the show-circuit life is easy. It isn't. The sheer physical work involved is often too much for people as they get older. Nor is there any assurance of a profitable day. Whereas in running a shop or a mail-order business one can look at the long perspective, those who do shows must make their money in a day or two. Otherwise, the trip is a loss.

On the other hand, you reach a new audience and, in many cases, a committed one. Anyone who has forked over three dollars or more in admission fees has at least indicated an interest in the field and the possible willingness to spend some money. Moreover, you not only have the opportunity to sell, you have the opportunity to advertise. Those who like your wares may later come to your shop or contact you if you deal privately or by mail order. Indeed, there are high-level dealers who will spend up to ten thousand dollars to do a major show *just* to make new contacts. If they sell something, that is an added bonus.

Once you have decided to give "show biz" a try, the next step is to select a favorable venue. For beginners, local shows are usually best. Trade papers and, often, your community newspaper should provide listings of these. As with auctions, a visit prior to enrolling is recommended.

Talk with dealers who have participated and find out what they think about the management and the crowd. Does the manager advertise the show properly, adhere to the terms of the contract with his or her dealers, and show an interest in their welfare? Remember, show managers have a somewhat ambivalent relationship to the dealers who set up at their shows. Managers usually make their money in two ways: from admissions and from booth rentals. In most cases, the latter is the major source of income. But the two are closely related. If dealers don't sell, they won't come back next time. Yet a manager's poor choice of dealer specialties, show location, or time of event may be the reason for the lack of action. If collectors don't like what the show has to offer, attendance will drop off, leading to further dealer withdrawals.

While there are many antiques shows, only a relatively small number prove suitable for a particular dealer. Try to make your selection carefully, and don't be afraid to drop out if the first experience indicates this isn't right for you or your merchandise. On the other hand, particularly with ground-breaking expositions (Arts and Crafts, 1950s, South American arts and crafts), it may take several years for a show to "get off the ground" and acquire an audience. There were quite a few dealers who left the New York Fall Antiques Show after the 1978 inaugural. The concept was new; their sales were few. Most would give their eyeteeth to be taken back today, now that the show has become one of the nation's most important.

Certain guidelines for selection can be followed. Try to conform to both the level and mix of a show. That is, if a show is primarily oriented to better-quality items, whatever their classification, don't apply for it if you don't feel that you have comparable merchandise. If you are accepted, you may be embarrassed—even if you sell (which you probably won't: people who attend better expositions are that much more discriminating).

Mix, which is the relationship among dealer specialties at a show, can be critical. If you sell country, you probably will not do well at a glass-and-jewelry show—even though the manager may urge you to sign up, since "you will be the only one in this field." Of course you will, but most customers for your goods will be somewhere else, and the buyers of Hummels, Victorian silver, and pressed glass will have little interest in your wares.

In fact, if you are a specialist in a particular field, such as toys or trains, you may decide to do a show (there are many) devoted only to your field. Showgoers may be fewer than at a general antiques-and-collectibles exposition, but they will be more serious. And it isn't the number of patrons that matters but their willingness to buy!

In most cases, the best rule is to make a modest start. Choose a small but respectable show that has been around for a few years and seems to have a merchandise mix compatible with yours. Avoid mall shows, unless they charge admission. Free entrance provides a lot of lookers but few buyers. Experienced dealers always say, "When you see the baby carriages, it's time to pack up." There are no children at the Winter Antiques Show. Patrons are there to buy, not to be entertained!

Avoid the so-called swap meets where everything from new products to fruit and vegetables and just plain junk is sold. You are an antiques dealer, a member of an ancient and honorable profession; your reputation is your major asset. It will not be enhanced by setting up next to someone selling plumbing supplies or reproduction Victorian chairs made in Taiwan.

Show Applications

It is more or less axiomatic that the easier an antiques or collectibles show is to get into, the less you will want to do it. With the exception of new shows, any show whose management must advertise for dealers or come around to other expositions passing out applications is, in most cases, to be avoided.

All the top shows have waiting lists, and with the "top-top" shows these are a mere formality. You can always apply for the Philadelphia or Houston shows, but you will also wait twenty years for admission unless you have the inside track—which involves money, business, and social connections. Not fair? Of course not, but who ever said things would be fair, least of all in what is essentially a luxury business?

Aim your sights a bit lower. There are many fine regional and local shows (the "waist" of our pyramid) that may be full at the moment but are always looking for new and exciting dealers. Show them you fit the bill.

Wherever possible, initial contact should be through a mutual friend: a member of the sponsoring charity or a dealer currently doing the show. If this is not possible, write a letter of inquiry. Your letter should be accompanied by a listing of the type of antiques and collectibles you would be displaying, shows you have done, and one or two good-quality photographs (35mm slides or color prints) of your shop or show setup.

The manager will either offer you the place for which you have applied, reject your application (usually on the ground that there is no available space), put you on a waiting list, or, if he (or she) has a circuit, suggest you do another of his shows. The last, known in the trade as "paying your dues," means taking part in a new or so-far unprofitable exposition as the price of admission to the desired show. If you really want to take part in the "name" show, it often pays to also do the less-desirable one.

If you are accepted, the next step is the contract. Any competent manager will have a standard written agreement covering each show. This will include the booth rental; the size of the space; what the management will furnish in the way of tables, dividing panels, lights or electrical outlets; and a notation of any special obligations required of the exhibitor—for example, to furnish drapery of a uniform color or not to pack up prior to close of the show (no matter how bad a day you have had!).

Watch for certain clauses. In regard to outdoor shows, for example, many promoters stipulate "rain or shine," which means that the show will go on even if the patrons must use rowboats! If you don't show up, you will not get a refund, no matter how bad the weather. Another paragraph common to the contracts covering better shows stipulates that no crafts objects or reproductions will be allowed. If you deal in such things, don't bother to bring them, as you will be required to remove them from the booth.

The ultimate application of this sanction is "vetting," a practice widespread in England but just getting a toehold in Canada and the United States. Under this procedure, recognized experts in each field examine the merchandise to be shown and remove anything that does not meet exposition standards—for example, a requirement that everything be pre-1900. Moreover, vetted shows usually require that all exhibits be clearly labeled as to age, origin, and other pertinent information, including price.

No one hoping to be a serious antiques or collectibles dealer should fear vetting. In fact, it is a clear benefit to both customer and dealer. Vetted merchandise carries a guarantee usually lacking in antiques transactions and therefore encourages active buying, especially by neophyte collectors.

Plainly marked prices, now required by law in the New York City art market, are protection against different prices being offered to different prospective customers and a blow against the snobbism prevalent in certain upper echelons of the antiques world.

The contract signed and returned (sometimes with full booth rental, otherwise with a deposit, the remainder to be collected during the course of the show), it is now time to prepare for the exposition.

Show Preparation and Display

Before signing a show contract you should have a pretty good idea of what things in your inventory will do best there. After all, you have looked over the show and talked to the dealers. You will have spotted the areas where you can undersell the competition, expand beyond what is usually available (adding less-costly silver plate where others are selling sterling, for example), or offer something spectacular that draws attention to your booth.

The latter is important. As a new dealer, you cannot hope for the best location. Do something to attract patrons—perhaps a booth emphasizing a single theme, such as the American eagle, or a single color, or one period, such as the Empire.

And do your homework. Come prepared with informative labels for your merchandise. Bring a stack of business cards (so that possible customers can find their way to your shop or home) and, if appropriate, a book of color photographs of all the wonderful things you had to leave behind. Some sharp dealers are even setting up film strips and slide shows to induce follow-up business.

Don't let your enthusiasm overcome your good judgment, though. If you have an eight-by-ten-foot or twelve-by-fourteen-foot booth, there is only so much you can squeeze into it. Your display should fit the allotted space. There are still a few dealers and collectors who love to rummage through piles of "stuff" looking for a treasure, but the current trend is toward sophistication. Booths today either have the warmth of a home, with a table set for the evening meal, or they look like art galleries, with the best pieces placed on white stands and blocks. Colors should not clash, and you should convey an impression of quality and pride in your offerings. After all, if you treat them like junk, why should someone else care to own them?

Like the visual impression made by your exhibit, your own attitude can be critical to show success. Unlike the relaxed shop situation, shows put great stress on both buyers and sellers. Patrons are faced with dozens or even hundreds of booths to see in a relatively short period of time. They are always looking down the aisle or over their shoulder. The visual impact of your display will draw them in, but *you* must hold and sell them. The hard sell is, however, rarely appropriate. A pleasant attitude, quick and informed response to inquiries, and the knowledge of when to leave people to do their own exploring are usually the marks of a top dealer. Don't follow people around pointing out the virtues of your merchandise or offering to reduce the price "just for" them. This is demeaning to everyone involved. Try to make customers feel at home (admittedly not easy to do when there are twenty people milling about in your space). If they like you, they will usually buy—now or later.

It is easy to maintain an alert, pleasant attitude through the first hours of a show, when excitement is high and the most active buyers, dealers, and serious collectors are scurrying through the hall. Six hours later, when it seems that no one will ever buy from you again and all the patrons have gone home for dinner, a certain lack of enthusiasm is inevitable.

But, it is now that you should be most on your toes. Half the competition is chatting among themselves, have abandoned their booths for the lunch room, or had so many predinner cocktails that they have lost all interest in the proceedings (a far more common situation than most dealers and managers will admit). It is at this time that some of the best sales and contacts are made, because now you can spend time with prospective customers and new collectors, advising them, encouraging their interests, and establishing their respect for your knowledge.

Don't worry too much about sales. Those will come. See the show as an opportunity to promote yourself and your merchandise. It is a form of advertising without equal, and those who take advantage of it will build a clientele where others fail.

Show Security

Security problems can be at their worst at an antiques and collectibles show, and they begin before the show does. Your first concern is transportation to the exposition site. Ideally, you should have two people loading and unloading so that if you are moving things from, say, a second-floor apartment to a van parked on the adjacent street, there will always be one person at each end.

This problem is exacerbated at the unloading (and reloading at show's end) stage, where you will often find that parking areas are located some distance from the exposition area and you have to make numerous trips to carry in your wares. This is a time of great confusion (frequently enhanced by the semi-darkness in which one works), and it is very easy for thieves to take objects or boxes from open vehicles. Rarely are these people fellow dealers. They are criminals who have discovered how vulnerable a dealer can be at this time.

Protect yourself by never leaving a vehicle unlocked or merchandise on the ground and, whenever possible, by employing two people so that one will be at the vehicle while the other is carrying things in. Never employ a "porter" who cannot prove he was hired by the show management. He may be working for himself!

The theft of antiques-loaded vans and trucks has become common enough (there have been two major incidents connected with New York's prestigious Winter Antiques Show in the past few years) that only the naïve now advertise their occupation by painting "Joe's Antiques" or something similar across their vehicles. The preferred method of transportation is a plain van with smoked windows (and *nothing* tied on top). Installation of an alarm system is also helpful.

Once you have everything safely in the exhibition area, set up your booth in a square or rectangle with only one exit (perhaps by arranging tables or furniture in this manner), and place your chair near that point. Avoid putting your purse or cashbox under a table. It seems safe there beneath the drapery, but that is just where a thief will look, and the cloth will screen his activity.

Keep your money on your person, and keep any valuable small items, such as jewelry or silver, in locked cases, which you will open for inspection upon request. Never show more than one piece of jewelry to one person at a time, and relock the case each time you remove a piece. A favorite sneak-thief trick is to work in pairs, one of whom distracts the dealer while the other goes into the open case.

Again, a single dealer in a booth is most vulnerable. If there are two of you, one can deal with most customers while the other remains near the exit, helpful and friendly but alert. Don't let this alertness veer into paranoia, however. If you seem to your customers nervous or overly suspicious, it will hurt your trade. Remember, you are going to lose a few things. Everyone does. It is part of the price of doing business. However, by following these few simple rules you can make it just difficult enough for the professional thief that he or she will go elsewhere.

Where shows run for more than a day, the management will provide overnight guards. Though there have been several incidents of theft (in at least one case with probable inside help), this security seems adequate for most objects. However, dealers handling quantities of silver and jewelry usually remove their cases every evening.

If something does disappear, don't look to the management

for compensation. Any well-drafted contract will contain a clause exempting the show manager from liability for any theft of or damage to exhibitors' goods, even if caused by the manager's negligence!

Packing for a Show

Finally, a few words about something that seems so simple and yet, if not properly done, can cause so many problems. Show packing is both art and science. Some dealers view it as a mystical experience: whatever their hands fall upon they toss into the van, confident that it will sell. Their packing involves stuffing a few wads of paper into a box or wrapping pieces in some old blankets.

Packing should be carefully thought out to allow for the maximum amount of merchandise in the space available. Breakables should be packed carefully in bubble pack and strong cardboard boxes or plastic milk containers (don't use Styrofoam popcorn—it will be all over the place). Furniture should be blanket-wrapped and separated so pieces do not rub together in transit. Ideally, you will include enough objects so that as things sell from your booth you can bring in more from the van. There is nothing like this constant flow of fresh "merch" to excite both customers and fellow dealers.

You should keep a complete list of all the antiques and collectibles you are taking to the show. When packing up at day's end, you can compare this with your sales book to make sure that nothing has been left behind or has disappeared.

And, most important, you must pack a kit containing the things you will need at the show: your sales or receipt book, bags and wrapping materials, your business cards, pens and pencils, a tape measure (so customers can measure furniture for their homes), light bulbs, a hammer, screwdriver, some nails and screws. Of course, you can always borrow from the management or other dealers, but it is much nicer and more professional to have your own.

Ultimately, the most professional dealers are the ones who do succeed at "show biz."

14.

SELLING FROM YOUR HOME

Certain antiques dealers have traditionally operated out of their homes and apartments. Specialists in rare books, antique guns, political memorabilia, and similar items for which there is no general public demand have found that since they have little "walk-in" trade there is no reason for them to maintain a shop.

However, with steady increases in the cost of doing business, many other dealers have joined their ranks, including generalists, furniture dealers, and others who, under different circumstances, might have preferred to have an open shop. Their major motivation, of course, is to save money on overhead. Rents have increased dramatically, not just in large cities but in desirable business areas throughout the nation.

When you're talking about not only a high monthly rent payment but, as is frequently the case today, a commercial "net lease" obligating the tenant to pay for such things as heat and a portion of the sewer, water, and similar taxes, it is understandable that alternatives are sought. Whether the alternative of selling from your home is suitable for you depends on several factors.

Who Should Sell from the House

What items you are selling should be a major element in any decision. There is no doubt that specialists can sell best from their homes. They depend least on the casual visitor, relying rather on a small but faithful clientele attracted through advertising, mail order, and, perhaps, show appearances. Also, if you have a busy show schedule—specialist or not—it may be unnecessary for you to maintain a shop. Customers whom you meet on the show circuit will visit your home—indeed, they will often be eager to, feeling that they are getting the "pick of the litter," being given a chance to buy before the items are offered at any exposition.

Much the same may be said for the mail-order salesperson. If you have an active mail-order business, some of your clients will inevitably "drop in" when they are in the area. In time, you will develop a steady patronage, especially if you send out periodic lists of what you have available. Selling from your home will in turn give you greater business flexibility; it will allow you to buy and sell things, such as furniture, which many mail-order dealers are reluctant to offer because of shipping problems.

Practical circumstances may also dictate your choice. If you handle quilts, snuffboxes, netsuke, or things similarly easy to store, you can certainly manage your business from a small house or even an apartment. If you deal in carousel horses, architectural artifacts, or furniture, you may simply not have enough room. Of course, I know a couple who ran a successful antique-furniture business from an apartment—the only thing not for sale there was the baby's crib!

Legal and Practical Considerations

There are also negative factors to be considered. You should determine what impact, if any, local ordinances and zoning laws may have on your business. Many communities do not allow businesses in residential areas. How strictly such regulations are enforced may depend in great part on the reactions of your neighbors and the outward manifestations of your activities. If pickers with six-wheelers start showing up on a regular basis, blocking the street and possibly endangering neighborhood children, it is quite possible that you will have complaints. On the other hand, so many people, especially in suburban areas, are running little desk-top businesses that most members of the community will overlook your venture if you will ignore theirs. Needless to say, though, business signs, yard displays, and other similar manifestations are an invitation to trouble. Discretion is advised.

The same thing may be said about apartment buildings. If you start using the passenger elevator regularly to transport your antiques, someone who has been inconvenienced or delayed is likely to complain. Slip the doorman a few bucks and use the service elevator.

If you rent, the landlord can also be a problem. Many standard leases forbid the tenant from running any sort of business on the premises. These clauses are subject to a variety of interpretations, and only an attorney familiar with local law and statutes would be able to determine if the occasional selling of antiques constituted a "business" within the meaning of the leasehold prohibition. As in dealing with the neighbors, discretion is the best path. You don't want to become involved with lawyers and legal questions, least of all with your landlord; but what he (or she) doesn't know won't hurt you. A low-key operation with a minimum of movement and activity should assure that. Again, a business in books, ephemera (paper goods such as trade cards, old magazines, movie posters, and the like), or small items attracts the least attention.

One of the best ways to avoid trouble with landlord or neighbors is to use a post-office box as a mailing address for your business correspondence. This essentially anonymous method of communication allows you to separate yourself from the use of the premises and avoids the delivery of business mail to your address.

Security

There is another good reason to use a post-office box as your mail drop. The most serious drawback to running an antiques and collectibles business out of your home is that you may run the risk of being burglarized or even robbed at gunpoint.

It is a sad fact of today's antiques world that dealers, largely ignored by the criminal element for decades, are now a subject of interest; some because they deal in items such as jewelry and precious metals that can easily be fenced, others because they sell things, such as fine paintings or early European porcelains, that may be stolen "on commission." The latter is an increasing problem. Thefts from dealers, private collections, museums, and historical societies are on the rise, and there is little doubt that they are often being masterminded by people with a good knowledge of antiques and collectibles. Shops and shows are certainly prime targets, but the private dealer operating out of his or her home is especially vulnerable. The premises are less visible than a shop or show and less subject to police protection.

Some years ago a Florida couple were murdered in their shop; and a violent theft during which a curator was bound and thrown down a flight of steps led to the recent sale of the well-known Perllman toy collection. This does not mean, of course, that one should not deal in antiques, whether from home or shop. What it does mean is that you should use good judgment, just as you would in any retail business.

A post-office box address will allow you to screen potential customers; so will an unlisted telephone number. While it is very difficult under various civil rights laws to exclude anyone from an open shop, no matter how dangerous he or she may look, a private home is another matter. You should allow no one into your house or apartment whom you cannot identify from a prior meeting at a show, through their response to your advertisements, or from the referral of another customer or dealer.

This does not, of course, ensure that you will have no problems, but it will substantially reduce the likelihood. Another wise precaution, especially if you handle objects of substantial value, is an alarm system. As discussed in chapter 12, "Selling from a Shop," these are costly and can almost always be bypassed. However, they are an effective deterrent to the crude break-and-enter burglar and will often make the more sophisticated operative look elsewhere. Much the same may be said of secure door and window locks and a large, mean-looking dog.

The problem of theft and how to deter it is certainly not unique to the home business. You will have similar concerns in a shop, cooperative, or mall. Many other aspects of the trade, when operated from a house or apartment, differ little from what you might expect to encounter in a shop on Main Street. At home you will still have to deal with questions of selection, packing and shipping, advertising, and restocking as your eager customers deplete your wares.

There is, however, one great difference, beyond the unquestionable financial savings. Prospective buyers almost always have a different attitude in your home. They are more respectful of you and of what you have to offer (just as you would be in their home), and they often seem to feel obligated to buy something simply because you have allowed them into your residence. This attitude can be encouraged by an offhand manner that implies that very few others are as fortunate as they. This both heightens their sense of privilege and makes them suspect that they are getting a first look at the merchandise. Indeed, this should be the case with your most valued steady customers.

One of the great advantages of dealing from your home is that you can control access. Those who have supported you with their patronage should be called and given a first shot at desirable things in their field of interest. Here you can avoid the unpleasant reaction sometimes aroused in latecomers by a SOLD sign at a show or in a shop. No one need know that you have rewarded the faithful.

One more aspect of home sales that bears mentioning is the effect of the business on your life and that of your family. Having relative strangers come through the house at odd hours can be disruptive, and I recommend that all business be done only by appointment and at times when it least impinges upon family life. Be sure to explain to children what is going on, since the sight of strangers carrying away what they thought were family furnishings can be upsetting.

Also, running a home-based business, particularly an active one, may keep you cooped up in the house for long periods. If you like to be out and about this may not be the best direction for your business to take. However, if it suits your personality and your schedule and can be adjusted to fit your family style, selling from the home provides one of the least-expensive avenues through which to enter the antiques business.

15.

SELLING BY MAIL

Mail-order merchandising is an old American tradition. Some say that the West was built and furnished and its people clothed and shod from the pages of the Montgomery Ward and Sears Roebuck catalogs, and there can be no doubt that the willingness of contemporary customers to buy "sight unseen" reflects the national confidence established through those bygone transactions.

For the dealer in antiques or collectibles, mail order offers a flexible method of reaching a new public. For some, it may be the only workable way to sell. For most, it can provide a handy adjunct to a shop or show-oriented business. In every case, the procedures to be followed are relatively simple, and, with a little patience and diligence, the field is likely to yield substantial profits with minimal risks.

An obvious advantage is that business overhead is kept to a minimum. Operating from your home, you not only do not pay extra rent, taxes, booth fees, or other expenses incidental to running a shop or traveling the show circuit, you also may be able to take a business tax deduction for the space set aside for storage, packing, and the answering of correspondence.

However, since the IRS keeps surprising us with new regulations, you will want to check this benefit with your attorney or accountant. It may be gone by the time you read this!

Mail order is so naturally related to an antiques or collectibles business that it is, in fact, hard to understand why everyone in the field doesn't do it. Experienced shopkeepers know that even at the best times there are quiet periods during which letters could be written, catalogs or price lists prepared, and packages wrapped. Those who follow the show circuit soon discover that they are selling to customers whom they will never see again (or at least not until they do this show next year) but who might respond favorably to a mail-order proposal. In fact, show contacts can have great potential; these clients have already gotten over the biggest hurdle—confidence. Having met you face-to-face and having bought something they are pleased with, they will be much more likely to respond to a mail-order solicitation than will someone who has been contacted "cold."

What to Sell

A dealer's natural reaction to the question of "What should I sell?" might be, "Well, just what I have always sold." But that may not be the most fruitful response. Mail order has certain natural limitations, and some things merchandise better in this way than others.

Furniture can be offered, but shipment presents problems. The most rapid shippers, UPS and the transcontinental bus lines, have size and weight limitations. Interstate truckers are more expensive and you will have to conform to their schedules, which often means that a client will not receive his or her purchase for several weeks or even months.

Many are reluctant to buy such things as precious gems and

jewelry through the mail, since even the best photographs can tell you little about an item's authenticity or quality. Antique guns and edged weapons can also present problems, due to state and federal restrictions on their shipment across state lines.

On the other hand, items that are relatively small, easily identified, and referrable to like items are ideal for the mail-order trade. For example, American tin toys of the 1930s can be readily sold, because they were mass produced, exist in substantial quantities, and can quickly be found in price guides or books specific to the toy field.

For many, specialization is the answer. The first mail-order antiques dealers limited their activities to narrow fields: Canton china (still an extremely popular area), Japanese netsuke, books with illuminated paintings, or something equally esoteric. The audience to which they appealed was a small but knowledgeable and eager one.

Today, dealers are apt to offer a more extensive menu. Those who sell Americana may have everything from quilts and coverlets to baskets, ceramics, and folk art. There are really few limits as to what can be sold through the mail. If you like dealing in a given area and can find an audience for your wares, go for it!

Building a Clientele

Critical to the success of your mail-order business is a list of likely buyers—not just a bunch of names clipped from a trade paper (though this is one way to start out) but what is known in the field as a "live" mailing list—a group of clients with a high purchase potential. These may be located in several ways.

If you run a shop or do shows you should keep the names of people who have bought from you or have specific requests.

Many dealers maintain a "guest log," which they urge visitors to sign, whether or not they buy. Clients identified in this manner have a fairly high purchase potential since they may have bought from you, liked what you sell, or at least will recall your shop's name.

By checking trade papers every week or month you can build up a group of collectors who run ads seeking specific things: fire-fighting memorabilia, matchbooks, canes, or what have you. These, too, should be added to your list, for they are serious prospects. However, you will find through experience that some are unwilling to pay market prices; these advertisements are often designed to attract "suckers" who do not know the value of what they have.

Finally, you will have a list of everyone who responds to your own advertisements in the trade publications. How many these are will depend on both the popularity of the field you have chosen for yourself and the effectiveness of your advertising.

Having made your choice, there is little you can do about its popularity. If you offer the public eighteenth-century English wine labels you are probably going to receive fewer responses than someone who is selling a broader category, such as Art Nouveau, Fiesta ware, or African art. On the other hand, such a specific ad will usually draw only the most interested responses, people who really are "looking to buy," as they say in the business.

The effectiveness of your advertising is quite another matter. One of the most important factors is photography. More and more contemporary advertisers recognize that a picture is truly "worth a thousand words." A good, sharp black-and-white image of one of the most appealing things you have available should highlight each ad. Don't make the mistake—as so many do—of trying to crowd your whole inventory into a single photograph. The only message the viewer gets is clutter.

Choose one or two good pieces and display them artistically. If you can't take good pictures, hire a professional. In the long run, it will be worth the expense.

Text is important, too. It should be accurate, of course, and describe as fully as possible what you are offering. Buyer confidence is enhanced by the feeling that you know what you are talking about. And, while there is dispute on this point among dealers, surveys make it clear that most would-be buyers prefer priced advertisements. They don't want to call just to find that they can't afford something. A phrase you should always include in your ad is "subject to prior sale"; this covers you with late callers after you have sold your lead piece to the first inquirer.

Every advertisement should also contain your telephone number, as serious buyers will always call. An address is less important; indeed, for security reasons you may prefer to list only a post office box, especially if you do not run an open shop.

Dealing with Customers

Selling to the mail-order customer is different from a face-to-face encounter, particularly if you have never met. Establishing a mood of confidence is most important. After all, you're asking the client to send you money for something he or she has never personally examined. I find that the business relationship is furthered by dealing with this problem directly and fairly.

First, I offer a ten-day money-back guarantee if the buyer does not feel (rightly or wrongly) that the piece is as described. Second, I send high-quality 35mm slides or Polaroid pictures of every item so that clients may examine them before making their final selections. Getting these returned can be a problem. It is amazing how inconsiderate some people can be even when provided with a stamped, self-addressed envelope. Of course, they are just damaging their own reputations. Nevertheless, the cost in those cases is justified by the vastly greater number of buyers who appreciate this service. Finally, I maintain a file card on each significant piece, listing such things as size, age, history or provenance, and, of course, damage. That way, when someone calls I can quickly pull out the card and provide him or her with answers to most of his or her questions.

If you follow these procedures, you should have few complaints and few returns. One thing to watch for, though— particularly with higher-priced items—is the dealer who will order something, run it around for a week trying to make a quick profit, then return it on some pretense. There aren't many of these people, and they soon develop a reputation in the field. Just scratch them off your list!

Packing and Shipping

Once a sale is made, your customer should immediately send a check or money order or, if you provide credit-card services, give you his or her card number. Most antiques dealers do not accept credit cards due to the three to five percent service charge on purchases payable by the shop owner, but if you wish to offer this alternative, get the details from your bank. In the case of a check, you should hold the merchandise (at least with new customers) until it has cleared the bank. Otherwise, you have little remedy against bad checks. This is customary in the trade, and few buyers will object to it.

Now comes the least attractive part of the business: packing and shipping. No one likes to do this; and, in fact, some people with large mail-order businesses hire others to do it for them. However, be aware that many will judge you on the basis of how well their purchase is packed and how quickly it arrives.

Each item should be packed with a copy of the invoice or bill of sale, while you retain another for your files. Some dealers send the client a third copy by regular mail. Packing should be done so as to assure maximum safety regardless of the value of the item involved.

Don't do your packing in old copies of the local newspaper. Shipping materials are part of the cost of doing business and should be the best available. Double-pack everything, don't overcrowd boxes, and be generous with the bubble pack or Styrofoam popcorn. If you also employ a competent carrier like UPS you will seldom suffer breakage. I have had only one instance of it in ten years.

Remember that common carriers have weight and size restrictions as well as, in some cases, limits on the maximum for which you can insure a given carton. By packing items in several boxes rather than a single one you can accommodate these restrictions.

Buyers should pay for both shipping and insurance. In the rare instance where they refuse coverage, you would be wise to insure on your own behalf. If anything happens in transit, you will be protected against a claim. Moreover, invoices should be explicit and should clearly describe the items sent so that if a claim must be made the damaged object can be readily identified and its value (usually the cost to the buyer) established.

Fortunately, all of these precautions will usually be for nothing. Most pieces get where they are going in good shape and are well received by the purchasers. If they didn't, mail order would not be the booming business that it is.

16.

AUCTION SELLING

*D*espite the touchy relationship that often exists between antiques dealers and the auction world, you should not dismiss the gallery as a way to make money. In fact, one class of dealer, the picker, has in recent years wholly embraced the auction system. With the high prices now being obtained at many houses, a growing number of "door knockers" and pickers have for the most part stopped selling to dealers, choosing instead to sell their finds directly through auction.

For the picker, this arrangement has one distinct advantage. Instead of carrying several dozen pieces around from shop to shop or calling twenty dealers and still ending up with some unsold merchandise, the picker simply turns it all over to his (or her) friendly auctioneer. In many cases, and assuredly if he is coming up with high-quality, quick-selling merchandise, the picker will receive a sizable preauction advance based on the estimated value of his goods. This is certainly superior to waiting thirty days after the gavel has fallen to get paid. And it also benefits the auctioneer, because it means that the picker, his pockets filled with money, will be out on the road again.

However, for most dealers the auction house plays a different role. It is, quite candidly, a place to dispose of things that for one reason or another have failed to sell. Neither dealers nor auctioneers care to discuss the matter, but many of the latter depend to a very great extent on the former for their merchandise.

As previously mentioned, knowledgeable buyers are always wary of the term "with additions" when it appears in an auction advertisement; this is often the tip-off to the fact that dealer goods are being recycled. Realistically, though, the number of antiques and collectibles available in the market at any one time is limited; and both auction houses and dealers recognize that a substantial percentage of what passes through the market is not "fresh" to it.

Moreover, what fails to sell in a shop or at a show may very well sell, and sell well, at auction. There are several reasons for this. Auction houses garner far more publicity and attract a much wider audience than most dealers can hope for. A wonderful but somewhat esoteric item that failed to attract due attention in your shop may be received with great enthusiasm by a broader and more sophisticated auction audience.

Then, too, price is always a consideration. If you own a fine piece, such as a Tiffany lamp or a sixteenth-century Tabriz carpet, you simply may not have clients who can afford it. An auction gallery can reach the right market.

Auction, though, can have a down side. Many dealers view it as a last resort and hope only to break even on their consignments so that the money will again be available for more fruitful purchases. This does not have to be the case. It is, to a great extent, a question of strategy. If you place the right things in the right places, you can make money at auction.

Auction Planning

The key to success in auction is determining what and where to sell. The "what" is very important. What are you selling—a rare and valuable piece for which you have no suitable local market, or an ordinary item that has been sitting around in the shop for a year? If it is the former, you must choose your auctioneer with great care. If you have a fine period French or Italian bronze or a scarce signed Gustav Stickley mission sideboard, the appropriate venue will probably be New York, Boston, or San Francisco. Placing it with a local or even regional auctioneer may not attract the battery of "heavy hitters" in the field that you want. You may even decide, if your treasure is a seventeenth-century Dutch clock or an important Renaissance drawing, that London or Geneva is the place for the hammer to fall.

The important thing is to know where an item will do best, and you cannot always count on your local auctioneer to come up with this information, because it is in his or her own interest to keep the piece at home, where he or she will earn a commission no matter what price is realized. Therefore, you may have to do your own research. Contact major national and international auction galleries to see if they are interested in what you have. They tend to be very direct (they can afford to be): if they estimate your lot as being worth less than one thousand dollars they will probably tell you to go elsewhere. If they show enthusiasm, you can be sure you have something of value.

If, on the other hand, you are just interested in getting your money out of an unfortunate acquisition, your best bet is a local or regional auctioneer. *But don't use one located nearby.* One of the common mistakes dealers make is to go up the road ten miles to sell their discards. Half the people and all the dealers in the audience at a nearby gallery will recognize your consignments. If you couldn't sell them, why should they try? If you want to get a decent return on your dollar, choose an auctioneer fifty or a hundred miles away. The extra travel time is worth it. You will be exposing the piece to an almost totally new audience.

Negotiating with the Auctioneer

Auctioneers are, in one sense, very different from antiques and collectibles dealers. If successful, they are cash rich and merchandise poor. Selling is less a problem for them than obtaining the items to sell. That means they are always ready to deal—how good the deal is will depend largely on what you have to offer.

The "deal" itself consists of several elements. First and foremost is the commission, the amount you must pay the auctioneer for selling your possessions. Depending on the circumstances detailed below, a commission will range from nothing to 20 or even 35 percent. Most auctioneers will initially insist on whatever is their standard, usually 10 to 15 percent, minus a traditional discount to the dealer trade, usually 2 to 5 percent.

Like everything else in the auction package, however, this is always negotiable. If you are offering a bunch of ordinary, shopworn items of the sort the auction gallery owner sees every day, chances are you will be glad to settle for the fifteen percent deal; glad, indeed, that the owner is even taking the stuff!

On the other hand, if you have good-quality, desirable items, especially something that has not been seen on the local market, don't be afraid to bargain. Major auction houses have taken collections for *no* commission, confident that they would make their money on the buyer's premium extracted from pieces selling at top prices. Remember, an auctioneer makes a lot more at 10 percent of five thousand dollars than 20 or 25 percent of one hundred dollars, and it usually takes no longer to sell the more expensive item than the less expensive one.

There are other areas for negotiation as well. Auction houses, especially the larger ones, will attempt to charge a fee—usually 1 percent of the selling price or low estimate—to cover insurance costs (everything should, of course, be insured from the time it leaves your premises until it is sold). There are also charges for shipping, and for photography if your piece or pieces are part of an illustrated catalog. Unless you are consigning the most ordinary items, always try to get these costs waived. Photography is for the benefit of both parties (just try to get your item photographed if the gallery thinks it is too ordinary!) and should, therefore, either be shared or borne by the auction house alone. After all, the photographer is on staff and gets paid by the week, not by the photograph. Insurance is based on the total policy premium, and you are just being asked to contribute. If you don't, someone less wise will.

Shipping is more of a problem. If possible, deliver things yourself. If not, and if the gallery will not waive the fee, see if you can find a common carrier like UPS to deliver for you. Chances are it will cost less than the auctioneer's charges.

Estimates and Reserves

Most auction houses do not place estimates on the things they sell. If you are dealing with one that does, you should bear in mind that estimates may influence bidder decisions as to the worth of a lot and are also usually tied in some way to the reserve price below which the lot will not be sold. The latter consideration is a most important one. The reserve is critical to most dealers, since they have paid for the merchandise (unlike many private consignors, who may have inherited their goodies or found them in the barn!). The reserve is the only protection you have against taking a big loss on your investment. You should insist on it.

Many auctioneers don't like reserves, because if a piece doesn't sell they don't earn a commission. On the other hand, their remedy is simply to know enough about the market to turn down pieces that they feel cannot reach the required figure. That way, no one gets hurt. Few auctioneers today maintain a blanket policy against reserves, and dealers are unwise to consign to those who do.

Determining estimates and reserves can, at times, border on the practice of witchcraft. Old-time hands will look at a piece, conjure up memories of a thousand sales, and say, "Oh, it might bring fifty to seventy-five dollars." Some young apprentice right out of a university fine-arts program will frantically dig through a hundred out-of-date auction catalogs and pontificate that the item will "surely bring five hundred to seven hundred fifty dollars."

Either could be right, but not both. The thing to bear in mind is that you are not just a consignor, you are an experienced antiques dealer. You know prices, and you know what you paid. Don't be intimidated. Insist on a reserve that will, at minimum, cover your cost plus auction fees. Above that figure mutual good judgment should prevail.

Once negotiations are completed you should receive a written contract, which sets out in full the terms of your agreement with the auction house and lists individually every item you have consigned. The sad story is that auction galleries, big and small, national and local, regularly lose or damage consignments. Theirs is a volume business, and mistakes are bound to happen. If something vanishes, you want to be in a position to prove without question that a piece was in the gallery's hands (and hence covered by its insurance) when the item went astray. The only way you can be sure of proof is to have a written and signed receipt.

Getting Paid

Today, more and more auction houses are moving to automated, computerized systems, which greatly expedite payment. The old days, when clerks recorded every sale in longhand, are rapidly vanishing. Some galleries are now prom-

ising payment within ten days of sale or even at the end of the
sale day. However, auctioneers have their own problems, one
of which is collecting on checks. What with bad checks,
bounced checks that clear the second time around, and steady
customers who have "arrangements" allowing for payment in
two weeks, most galleries should not really be expected to
make payment in less than three to four weeks.

On the other hand, anything much beyond this is not right.
It is your money the auctioneer is playing with, and you need
it at least as badly as he (or she) does. Don't let him finance his
business with your funds. When thirty days have passed, get
on the telephone.

Finally, bear in mind that you too can have the deal the
pickers get. If you are offering quality merchandise, you can ask
for an advance against the prospective auction returns. Both
Sotheby's and Christie's are now doing this with major consignors as a matter of policy (it encourages consignments), and
any substantial auctioneer with a pocketful of cash will be
amenable to such a deal. He might even suggest it if he thinks
you have a pipeline to good merchandise.

The bottom line with the auction world is that it is a free-
wheeling extravaganza where the most outrageous demands
might be satisfied and the most reasonable requests ignored.
Be the squeaky wheel, and you will get the grease. Be silent
and reasonable, and you will be rolled over.

17.

SPIN-OFF ACTIVITIES

How many times have you gone into an antiques shop and found the proprietor watching television, reading a trashy novel, or just looking off into space? Often enough, I'll wager, that you may have wondered how anyone could stand to be so bored. Yet we all know that the antiques and collectibles field is far from boring. It is, in fact, one of the most exciting and educational areas of endeavor. The problem is that many dealers, when confronted with the hours between customers—which are inevitable at any level of the business (no one sells constantly)—seem at a loss as to what to do with themselves.

Yet there are many business-related activities that will not only occupy one's time and increase one's knowledge of the field but will also earn money . . . the money that might make the difference between success and failure.

Refinishing and Restoration

Particularly in rural regions and smaller communities, there is a dearth of competent restorers. The field is an extremely broad one, ranging from simple dip stripping of furniture to the subtle arts of clock and jewelry repair. The necessary skills may be learned in a few days from a book or on-the-job training or may require months or even years of application. Whatever the case, all elements of refinishing and restoration share the common virtue of being crafts that are much in demand, are well paid, and can be conducted in the home or shop, preferably during time that can be spared from one's antiques and collectibles business.

Refinishing old and not-so-old furniture has become such an important business that it has been franchised. There are now several national chains offering dealerships in the field, and information on these may be obtained from the various antiques publications.

"Dipping," as dip stripping is often known, involves the use of caustic chemicals in vats large enough to accommodate sizable pieces of furniture. It therefore requires a substantial space set apart from your shop or home and, consequently, it is not for everyone. Moreover, the expenditures involved for materials and equipment mean you would have to operate the business on a fairly large scale to make it profitable.

On the other hand, dry stripping (hand scraping of later layers of paint to reach an original surface), heat-gun stripping, and the stripping of individual pieces employing any one of the many liquid or semiliquid removers can be done on a limited scale in a smaller space and with little or no overhead.

Further, hand stripping, and subsequent application of a hand-rubbed finish (where necessary), not only requires greater time, skills, and diligence than vat dipping but is also a much more highly paid field. And if you love to handle fine furniture, this may be just the thing for you. Few knowledgeable people will submit anything more valuable than turn-of-the-century oak or "used" furniture to the vats, whereas hand strippers often get to work with good eighteenth- and nineteenth-century pieces.

A related skill is restoring painted furniture surfaces. Many grained or decoratively painted pieces are in need of sophisticated restoration, which calls for artistic skill as well as technical knowledge of the proper period paints. So great is the demand for restorers with this talent that at least one museum, The Museum of American Folk Art, in New York City, now offers a course in marbleizing and grain painting.

Beyond the field of furniture lies a virtually unlimited area for the restorer. Most people who become restorers specialize in one or two areas, usually ones in which they have a collecting interest. Thus, a doll enthusiast and dealer will learn to stuff cloth bodies, restring dolls, and perhaps even cast papier-mâché or composition heads. A lover of old textiles may become skilled at reweaving damaged hooked rugs or cleaning and repiecing (with period fabrics) early quilts. Whatever your field of interest in antiques and collectibles, you can be sure that there is need for competent restorers. Your work will fill that time between shows or sales, enable you to learn even more about the things you love, and—often most important—provide additional income.

Chair Seating and Upholstering

A related and extremely popular part-time activity is chair seating. Many chairs, both antique and modern, have seats of fabric or natural materials that must be periodically restored. The most common fabric is woven cotton tape of the sort used on Shaker chairs, while natural materials include ash or hickory splint, natural or paper rush, Oriental split cane, and rawhide (generally employed only on nineteenth-century western and southwestern seats).

All but the rawhide may be obtained from commercial suppliers, and the procedure involved is in most cases so uncomplicated as to allow you, for example, to put a tape or splint seat in a chair while watching television! There are, however, exceptions. Repairing a seat of natural rush (really water-soaked cattail leaves) is a sloppy and time-consuming task, while the tedium involved in caning a chair back or seat is reflected in the way the job is priced . . . by the inch!

There are several sources for chair-seating materials, all of which advertise in antiques and crafts publications. These firms also provide, either free of charge or for a nominal sum, simple instructions for the installation of the more common seats.

Book Sales

One of the most important needs of all collectors and dealers is knowledge of their fields of interest, yet in most areas of the country it is extremely difficult to obtain authoritative texts in the antiques and collectibles field. The number of independent book dealers (those who really know and love books and who are most likely to stock serious studies of anything from Sung dynasty bronzes to Art Deco waffle irons) has dwindled to less than five thousand nationwide. As these dealers vanish, they are either not replaced at all (one can hardly call the rows of cheap paperbacks in shopping centers a "book store") or their place is taken by a national-chain bookstore.

More and more, the latter offer nothing in the antiques and collectibles line other than price guides and a few mediocre, superficial texts on such amorphous topics as "country," "relics," "oak," and the like by authors whose names might well be (and sometimes are) "anonymous." If you want authoritative, well-researched books written by nationally recognized authors and published by major commercial or university presses, you often must resort to mail order.

Commercial publishers must, in part, be blamed for this situation; for years they have refused to accept wholesale orders of less than several dozen copies of a single title, making it difficult for small sellers to do business with them. Now, however, faced with a dwindling number of privately owned book stores and unwilling to accept the high discounts demanded by the chains, they are turning to an unlikely outlet: the antiques and collectibles dealer.

You can obtain a half-dozen or a dozen copies of one or more books in the antiques and collectibles field at the same discount offered to a bookstore and with the same return policy. This allows you to offer your serious buyers the opportunity to purchase important texts otherwise available to them only through the mail. Not only do you give these clients the chance to educate themselves in ways that, if you carry antiques or collectibles of value, cannot help but improve your business, you also further establish yourself as a knowledgeable dealer rather than just another "merch" flogger.

Those who come to buy antiques will buy books. Those who come to buy books will, sooner or later, also buy antiques. The relationship is a natural one and one that should in time establish your reputation throughout the community in which you do business. Will you make money on your book sales? Yes, but not any significant amount. The thirty to fifty percent markup on a dozen or so titles may pay the month's electric bill. Advertising and image enhancement, not profits, are the major reasons for book sales.

Prop Rentals

In larger cities, many dealers are able to increase substantially their earnings through renting antiques and collectibles for use as props in everything from movie and television productions to professional theater and college productions to retail-store display.

The rule of thumb in the trade is "every three rentals is a sale." In other words, each time you rent a piece of furniture or another object to a television studio or a local department store you should charge approximately thirty-three percent of the retail selling price of that object. Moreover, rentals should be for fixed periods. Ideally, a day, a week, or a month is best. Usually, the per-day rental declines as the overall length of the rental increases, but there are really no fixed rules in this area. One standard, however, is that (except for a school or amateur theatrical group) a month's rental should at least equal the original cost of most pieces.

If this seems high, bear in mind that rentals are rough on the merchandise. Stage, movie, and television crews are notoriously hard on props, drawing no distinctions between antiques and used furniture. In most cases, things will come back the worse for wear.

Therefore, anything you rent should be insured, at the renter's expense (and with you as beneficiary), for its retail value. Moreover, all rentals should be pursuant to a written agreement setting out the charges, duration of use, responsibility for pickup and delivery, insurance, and proper credit. This last thing is especially important. Make sure that you always get credit on the playbill, credit lines, or advertising. A phrase like "Period furnishings courtesy of Elaine's Antiques" is among the best advertising you can get.

Interior Decoration

Interior decorators are both bane and blessing to the antiques dealer. Many know nothing about antiques and have no desire to learn. Their only interest is in a look, often grotesque, which they have picked up from a fashionable magazine and then sold to their unknowing client. Like as not, they will ask you to strip a fine old finish off a piece of eighteenth-century furniture or repaint it to match "their" decor.

On the other hand, the decorator frequently is a wonderful customer freely spending his or her client's funds for things you thought would never leave the shop. Inevitably, though, as you work with these people the thought will cross your mind that you could do the job better and provide the client far better quality for the money. You are probably right!

Many, though certainly not all, antiques and collectibles dealers have both the taste and the flair for design required of an interior decorator. And, unlike the decorator, they also have an in-depth knowledge of the field. If you are interested in linking your business to interior decoration, bear in mind that the fields, though related, are dissimilar in many ways. As an antiques and collectibles dealer, your clientele consists primarily of people interested in acquiring objects. The interior decorator deals with people who are interested in a "look" to which the objects, no matter how precious, are secondary.

Reaching this clientele involves advertising not in antiques publications but in those catering to the home-decorating trade, builders, and architects. Look around your community. Who is building new homes? Who is doing the renovation? Who is sponsoring the interior-design open houses and showcases? These are the people you want to approach, and their publications are the ones in which you want to advertise.

Selling Architectural Artifacts

Closely related to interior decoration is the booming business in architectural artifacts, a term that encompasses the various odds and ends—from cast-iron fences and eighteenth-century paneled doors to Victorian fretsawn gingerbread trim and demilune barn windows—that accumulate when old structures are torn down or remodeled.

Larger pieces are incorporated into new or old houses, while smaller ones, such as colored-glass windows or carved and painted fence-post finials, may be displayed individually as works of art. It is the latter that are handled most often by antiques dealers. The large scale of most architectural artifacts requires storage facilities beyond the means of most dealers in the trade.

However, you *can* be successful in the architectural trade. There are two essentials. First, you need a large space in which to store your finds. Second, you must be in an area, preferably a sizable but decaying city, where raw material is readily and inexpensively available. If you do find yourself in this position, your costs will be relatively low. By making purchase arrangements with contractors in charge of demolitions, you should be able to obtain your "raw materials" quite inexpensively. Smaller items can be kept for stock or sold to the folk-art specialists who are most interested in this material. Larger pieces can be offered through the pages of antiques, architectural, and interior design publications to people who are building new homes or refurbishing old ones and to the designers of businesses such as restaurants and boutiques, who have a constant need for such trendy stuff.

The field of architectural artifacts is one of the most rapidly expanding segments of the antiques and collectibles world. If you are in a position to take advantage of current design trends, this is where you may really make your fortune!

18.

PROMOTION

Promotion is absolutely critical to the success of any antiques endeavor, but especially to shop or show businesses. No matter how high quality your merchandise may be and how knowledgeable and ethical you are, if people don't know you and feel that it is important to buy from you, you will never do well. There are a vast number of dealers active in today's antiques and collectibles world. It is your job to distinguish yourself from the competition. When collectors in your area think of a category of antiques or collectibles, of a particular type of shop, or of a certain shopping area, they should be thinking of you.

Yet, traditionally, advertising and self-promotion have never played a major part in the antiques world. In the "good old days," dealers sat in their shops and waited for seasoned collectors, who then spread the word about a dealer's merchandise, knowledge, and integrity. It took years to build up a favorable reputation, and, once established, this reputation would be maintained for generations in a respected family business.

Things are much different today. There are far more collectors, many of whom know little about the antiques and collectibles they covet and most of whom are accustomed to and easily swayed by media barrages. It is now commonplace for young dealers with little knowledge but much money to leap to the top of the business pyramid by placing a few full-page color advertisements in *The Magazine Antiques* and spending outrageously high sums at well-publicized auctions. The ability to spend money freely has become equated with knowledge and experience.

This easy course to the top is, unfortunately, not available to most dealers. For them, self-promotion and the establishment of a business reputation must be achieved on a limited budget and over a period of time. There are, however, ways to lighten one's task.

Advertising

The first and foremost manner of calling public attention to one's business is through paid advertising. But beware: the wrong sort of advertising is little better than none at all. Placement is key. Spend your ad money on the publications that reach the audience you want to attract.

To take an obvious example, if you are a specialist dealing only in French and German dolls, you would want to advertise in one or more of the magazines aimed at doll collectors. Advertisements in a general antiques publication would probably be of little value, and money spent on space in a publication narrowly focused on another field, such as folk art or early tools, would be money thrown away.

Target your audience. If you sell expensive items, advertise only in media that reach a public that can afford your prices. If you count heavily on local walk-in trade, advertise locally. On the other hand, if you do a national mail-order business and do not maintain an open shop, you probably will not need local coverage.

By no means do you have to confine yourself to the traditional antiques and collectibles publications. Be a little creative and you will find customers in all sorts of places. If you offer country furniture and accessories, advertisements in traditional home magazines, such as *Better Homes and Gardens*, may open up a new market. Those who deal in architectural remnants may attract customers through the pages of *Architectural Digest* or magazines aimed at builders, interior designers, and urban planners.

Be flexible and be willing to change direction if your current advertising doesn't seem to be doing the job. It is easy to monitor the effectiveness of your ads. When people come into your shop or show booth or call you for a business appointment, ask them where they heard of you. If, over a period of four to six months, you find that advertisements in certain media are drawing little response, pull them and look elsewhere. It's your money, and you should spend it in the most beneficial way.

Writing the Ad

It is not enough to advertise; your advertising must be effective. Remember, as far as the public is concerned, your ads are you. You want to make the best possible public presentation. That means you should use photography wherever possible, and that photography should be of good quality. Choose which pieces to advertise for their quality and for their ability to represent accurately your overall taste and stock. Photographic captions should be clear, concise, and accurate. The last thing you want to do is give the impression that you don't know what you have; nothing turns off a knowledgeable collector faster— unless it is the use of such silly, boastful terms as "antiquarian" or "America's leading authority on Federal furniture." Whenever possible, link your offering to an example found in a

respected publication in the field (*not* a price guide); for instance, when you advertise a weathervane, you could say "for
a similar example see figure 102, Bishop's, *American Folk
Sculpture.*"

In most cases, you will be submitting black-and-white photographs, and these should be sharp and clear, of professional
quality. The reproduction in most antiques tabloids is none too
good. The better the image you give them, the better the
result. Photographs should be of a single object or of a small
group, tastefully arranged. One of the biggest mistakes advertisers make is to try to put their whole shop in the picture! The
result is a mess. Remember, potential buyers want to *see* what
they are considering.

Pricing is always a big issue. Many dealers will never price
their ads, because they don't want the competition (who may
have been present when they bought the piece at auction or
who may have sold it to them) to know their markup. On the
other hand, there are collectors who, as a matter of principle,
won't buy from unpriced advertisements. My own feeling is
that the inclusion of prices is both proper and often saves time
and effort (people who can't afford the piece won't call).

When you prepare your ad, always put in a disclaimer, such
as "Subject to prior sale," to cover the eventuality that the piece
is sold to the first caller or prior to the advertisement coming
out. Some dealers use this to cover themselves when they
illustrate a fine piece from their own private collection; they
have no intention of selling it but are simply employing it to
impress the public with the quality of their stock. I don't
advocate this sort of misrepresentation, but it is rather widely
practiced.

Newspapers and trade magazines are not the only media
available to advertisers. The use of radio and television time
slots to promote antiques malls, shows, and, in rare cases,
individual shops is becoming popular, particularly in the
West, where collectors may be induced to drive a hundred

miles to visit a popular group shop. The major sticking point here is generally money. Advertising rates are usually prohibitive unless the promotion is a joint one, paid for by several dealers.

A less costly cooperative promotion is an inexpensive flyer showing a map of your area and listing all the local antiques shops along with a brief description of their hours, specialties, and so on. Paid for jointly and available at each shop in the area, such a flyer turns one dealer's fortune into every dealer's fortune as prospective buyers follow the "antiques trail" from shop to shop.

Finally, bear in mind that in the long run any advertisement is less important for the immediate sales it may generate than for what it contributes to the total impression of you and your business. This is important in mail order but much more important if you are a shop or show dealer.

Inexpensive Self-promotion

A mistake that many dealers make is to assume that paid advertisements are the only way to the public's heart. Therefore, if they lack the funds for a media blitz they feel they are forever doomed to obscurity. Not so. There are many ways of bringing your business to public attention that will cost you little or nothing. One is cultivating the patronage of prominent local citizens. Wealth and position, of course, provide an immediate advantage here. There are New York City dealers and decorators who have existed for years on family contacts.

Yet, lacking these, it is still possible to bring attention to your business. One way is through charity. Never turn down representatives of local charities, no matter how obscure, when they ask to place signs in your windows in support of their fund-raising drives or ask for a subscription to an antiques-show brochure. Always be ready to volunteer as an appraiser at a show or "heirloom-appraisal session" for a worthy cause. Offer to donate a decent antique or collectible (not some "dog" that everyone in town has seen for months in your shop!) as a door prize at charitable events.

People involved in charitable funding well understand the adage, "one hand washes the other." If you support them, they will support you. With the increasing use of antiques shows, auctions, and appraisal sessions in fund-raising, opportunities in this area can only increase.

Also take advantage of chances to display your knowledge and at the same time contact potential customers. One of the best means to this end is through teaching. Most communities have adult education programs, at either the high school or collegiate level, and most of these programs would be interested in offering courses on antiques and collectibles. The reason is simply economic. Such courses almost always have a large audience.

Draw up a proposal for a course in your field of expertise and see if you can't sell it to the administration. The course outline and your prior experience will be important factors in their decision, but the final arbitrators will be the students. If you can draw and hold a good group, you are set for life!

Teaching such a course offers two advantages. Each semester you will be reaching a new group of collectors and dealers, all of whom are potential customers. Moreover, by teaching, you establish yourself as a local expert, which will give you a definite edge on the competition. You won't make much money from the course itself; adult-education instructors are never very well paid, but, after all, that isn't the reason you are teaching.

More difficult to arrange but that much more beneficial is a position writing articles on antiques and collectibles for local newspapers or hosting a talk show on collecting for the local radio or television station. With increasing centralization of these media, it is extremely hard to break into the field, but if you have an important contact you might be able to do it. The audience reached this way is, of course, considerable.

It should also be noted that the antiques tabloids offer opportunities for free as well as paid advertising. Most of the monthly papers will accept without charge brief notices on special exhibits, sales, and shop relocations. Some will even publish thinly disguised self-promotion if it is couched in scholarly terms. Say you are holding an exhibition of patriotic memorabilia to coincide with the July 4th holiday. An article on the significance of the date and the historical interest of the memorabilia displayed will often slip through, even though everything in your exhibit is for sale.

One of the newest promotional gimmicks employed at the financial top of the market is the museum tie-in. A dealer will enlist a museum in a joint exhibition displaying both museum-owned examples and objects from his (or her) own stock. The latter will not usually be for sale at the museum (that would be *too* boorish!), but they soon will be, in the dealer's shop, and in the meantime, the dealer employs the credibility of the museum in promoting his own name and merchandise.

Frankly, I find such tactics appalling and am at a loss to understand why reputable institutions lend their names to the practice, but I call it to your attention as an example of the extremes to which self-promotion may be carried.

Extremes are usually to be avoided, for, while the purpose of advertising and promotion is to bring public attention to you and your business, the attention should be favorable and non-controversial. There is a saying that "there is no such thing as *bad* publicity," and in some fields—entertainment and the like—that may be true. But not so in antiques. Avoid anything that smacks too much of the marketplace. Gentility has always been a hallmark of the antiques and collectibles trade, and the dealer should not strive to emulate the used-car salesman.

In the long run, your reputation will be your best recommendation to the public. No matter how flashy your advertising may be or how much money you pour into the media, if you get a reputation for frivolousness, questionable dealings, or inadequate knowledge of the field in which you profess to be an expert, customers will turn away from you. Reputation is forever!

19·

APPRAISING

Since an appraiser is one who places values on objects, every antiques dealer is already one, by definition. After all, what we do each day is evaluate those items offered to us and determine whether or not they can be sold at sufficient profit to justify purchase. The prices we place on them reflect our appraisal of their retail market value.

Of course, the field of appraising is much broader than this. There are professionals who appraise real estate, businesses, and a wide variety of nonantiques, such as automobiles, machinery, and even herds of cattle. However, when you ask most people about appraisers they tend to associate them with the antiques and collectibles world. It is in this area that the most publicity, favorable and unfavorable, has been generated.

Favorable notice often comes from "appraisal days," sponsored either by auction houses (who are seeking to acquire consignments) or local historical societies or charitable groups, at which rare and valuable objects are discovered. Unfavorable notice has arisen because of IRS claims against individuals who have overvalued—with the help of an appraiser—art or antiques given as charitable deductions to museums and the like. In either case, the results have tended to promote an image of the appraiser as a magician who can create value in seemingly worthless items.

Of course that isn't so. The value is either there or it is not. The appraiser only recognizes it on the basis of his or her experience, and, in any case, an appraisal is just an educated guess based on such things as auction results, price guides, and dealer information as to the likely market value at a given time.

Who Is an Appraiser?

Under the present state and federal law, anyone who wishes to hold himself or herself out to the public as an appraiser becomes one. There are no qualifying or licensing procedures, and the terms "qualified" or "certified" used by certain appraisers are nothing more than a form of self-promotion.

There are several organizations to which appraisers may belong and which, in varying degrees, attempt to educate their members and control abuses. On the national level there are the American Society of Appraisers and the International Society of Appraisers. Regional organizations include such groups as the New England Appraisers' Association, the Antique Appraisal Association of America (West Coast), and the Mid-Am Antique Appraisers Association (midwestern area). All of these latter organizations regularly advertise for recruits in the various trade publications.

All make an attempt to promote knowledge and integrity in the field. Among the larger groups, there recently has been a movement toward educational programs, including required courses leading to a form of "certification" within the organization. However, this has no *legal* significance and is not necessarily a guarantee of either competence or ethics. Thus, if appraising interests you, there is no legal prohibition to your entering the field, and, as an antiques and collectibles dealer, you will usually find your services in demand.

Types of Appraisals

Appraisers are employed for several reasons; chief among these are insurance evaluations, estate appraisals, and the determination of fair market value in anticipation of a sale. Curiously, these are three very different undertakings. Determining the fair market value is the most straightforward. It assumes a situation with a willing buyer and a willing seller, and neither has any unusual compulsion to act within any specific period of time. This is essentially the situation one would find at an antiques show, in a shop, or generally at auction; and the fair market value would be what we might refer to as a retail sales price.

Insurance appraisals have a different result. Given the increasing market values of antiques and collectibles as well as the constant danger of fire, theft, earthquake, tornado, and other natural disasters, many collectors are very concerned about having adequate insurance coverage. Insurance companies will require an evaluation as a condition for issuing a policy, and this same appraisal will be an important tool in negotiating a settlement with the insurer if a loss is suffered.

An insurance appraisal seeks to determine the "replacement" value of a lost or destroyed antique. This may exceed the fair market value, because the insured is entitled to have the item replaced immediately rather than waiting for the insurer to find the best deal. Thus, there is an eager buyer with a compulsion to purchase—often leading to the payment of a higher-than-market price.

Estate appraisals, which are generally necessary when the estate is required by law or because of a will to be divided on specific terms among several heirs or when the estate is large enough to require filing of a federal estate tax return, reflect a different sort of fair market value. Here it is in the interest of the heirs, the executor or administrator of the estate, and, most importantly, the federal and state tax authorities that the estate be liquidated and all bequests and taxes quickly paid. Consequently, items may be valued at a "distress-sale" level, with a seller eager to sell and buyers taking advantage of this to pay less.

Which of these three situations you find yourself in will be reflected not only in the appraised values you arrive at but also, to some extent, in your appraisal methodology.

Appraisal Procedures

Accuracy and documentation are the secrets of successful appraisals, and the road to these begins before the appraisal is undertaken. Equipment is very important. Appraisers often work under very difficult conditions. Ideally, the things to be appraised would be in well-lighted rooms; readily accessible; would have detailed histories of purchase, including original bills of sale; and would be common enough in nature that prices could be quickly determined. The ideal is seldom realized!

When you're going on an appraising job, always assume the worst. Carry a kit of "tools" to make your work easier. This should include two flashlights, one large, the other a small penlight to see into places where you can't get the larger one; a tape measure (for identification by measurement); a magnet for determining the nature of metals; a large magnifying glass and a tiny jeweler's loop; a set of scales for weighing precious metals; a black light for inspecting paintings, glass, and porcelain; and a camera for photographing important pieces.

To record your findings you will need a large notebook and several pens or pencils or, better yet, a tape recorder. Talking into a tape recorder is faster than writing, allows for much more detailed commentary, and avoids the problem of your having later to decipher the notes you took in such haste.

Appraisals of any size should be conducted in a rational

manner, area by area. Start with one room and record each item to be appraised there, then move on to the next. Don't jump around. Examine objects carefully, recording both what you recognize about them and what you don't. Should there have been finials on that highboy? What sort of glass is that, blown or pressed? Don't be disturbed if you can't price, or don't even recognize, something; it happens to everyone. Whatever you do, don't fake it. Some of the worst problems appraisers get themselves into come from guessing about identification or values because they are too lazy to check or don't want to admit they don't know.

As a general rule, the more valuable a piece, the more carefully it should be examined and documented. An eighteenth-century desk, for example, should be measured, and you should note its type of wood (both primary and secondary) as well as style; construction techniques, such as dovetailing, wrought nails, whether hardware is original or replacement; and, of course, all damage and restoration.

How a knowledgeable appraiser handles restoration usually reflects the type of evaluation he or she is doing. If the desk in our example had replaced feet, someone doing an estate appraisal might make much of this defect in order to justify a low valuation that is desired for tax purposes, for example. On the other hand, if he were appraising for insurance purposes, he might emphasize the high quality of the restoration (particularly if, as is often the case, his client bought the piece not realizing the feet were not original!) as support for a substantial insurance value.

Note, though, that in either case it is a matter of emphasis. To conceal deliberately a defect or to create one where none exists is unethical and probably illegal.

All important pieces should also be photographed. Some insurers require this, and your client certainly will want a visual record in case of total loss through theft or fire. Good-quality pictures also allow you to reexamine a piece when writing up

your report without having to go back to the scene of the
appraisal. A Polaroid-type camera is ideal for this work, as you
can develop the film immediately and see if it is adequate. A
roll of overdeveloped or underdeveloped film will be of little
help to you!

Try to collect as much information as you can from the
owner about the provenance of the things being appraised.
Documentation, for example, showing that an otherwise-
ordinary bracelet was owned by a European head of state is
likely to increase its worth greatly. On the other hand, vague
statements that something is "two hundred years old" or "very
valuable" must be taken with a grain of salt. You are the
appraiser, and you are hired to make the evaluations based on
your experience, not just to confirm an owner's idea as to what
something is worth.

Writing the Appraisal Report

Once you have examined everything you have been hired to
appraise, it is time to prepare your report. This should be done
at least in triplicate, with a copy for your client, one for your
files (where it should be retained for at least four years against
the possibility of claims or litigation), and at least one other to
be furnished at the client's request to a third party, such as an
insurance company or taxing authority. Remember that this is
a confidential document. Under no circumstances should it be
shown or given to others without the *written* consent of the
client for whom the appraisal was done.

The form of the appraisal document varies from individual
to individual, but it should have an introductory clause indi-
cating when, where, and for what purpose the appraisal was
done, as well as a concluding paragraph in which you set out
your qualifications. The latter is very important and should

include your years of experience in the field, any books or articles you have written, courses taught or attended, and anything else that tends to establish your expertise. The more impressive your résumé, the less likely that your evaluations will be challenged by either an insurance company or the IRS.

The appraisal should be dated and signed by you (and by any other person you may have called in for consultation) and should be put in a high-quality binder. It is a legal document, and it should look like one. Never skimp on the quality of the materials used. They represent you.

Appraisals of the individual items within the document should be complete enough both to identify the item and to justify your evaluation. Remember, three years from now you will recall little of this transaction, so you should describe the appearance, size, shape, color, provenance, condition, and age of each piece in sufficient detail that not only you but others can visualize it. If you have a photograph, it should be attached to the same page.

How much space all this will take depends on the specific object. Most things can be adequately described in two or three paragraphs. An important piece, or one that you see as possibly being at issue somewhere down the line, may justify a page or more. Err on the side of thoroughness. The better your evaluations, the less likely they are to be challenged; and, if challenged, the more likely they are to be upheld.

Legal Aspects of Appraisals

Readers may already have noted my emphasis on preparing to defend your appraisals. This is an important aspect of the field and one often passed over too lightly by writers on the subject. It is fair to state flatly that if you do a substantial number of appraisals (say, several hundred a year), sooner or later, no matter how thorough and knowledgeable you are, you will find yourself embroiled in litigation.

Insurance companies love to collect premiums but may not be so enthusiastic about settling claims, especially for the full amount for which an item is insured. If a substantial sum is involved, they will probably bring in another appraiser, either to look at the piece (if it is available) or to attempt to poke holes in your appraisal. This may ultimately lead to an arbitration hearing (if that is provided for in the policy), or even a lawsuit by the insured against the insurance company. In either case, you are likely to be called upon to defend your appraisal. If this thought sends chills up your spine, there is probably not enough money to be made in the field to justify the risk.

Much the same may be said of other appraisal areas. An estate-tax evaluation may be challenged as too low by the appropriate taxing authority, or the IRS may question the legitimacy of an appraisal done to fix the worth of art or other items deducted as a charitable contribution. In either case, if the client ends up in tax court, you will be right there with him or her.

As I have said, careful documentation and accurate appraisals will go a long way toward avoiding such disputes or, where they do occur, having them resolved in your client's favor. Another way of protecting yourself is to limit your work to areas where you are especially knowledgeable. No one can know every category of antiques and collectibles. When you find that you must evaluate items with which you are unfamiliar and about which you still do not feel adequately knowledgeable, even after studying the appropriate references, by all means, bring in a specialist. Sure, you will have to split your fee, but you will be giving your client the best service and protecting yourself as well. There may even be times when you will have to turn an entire job over to someone else because you just aren't equipped to handle it. But it is better to do that than to find yourself having to defend an inadequate appraisal in court.

Fees

Now the good news! Yes, it is possible to make substantial sums as an appraiser, either on a full-time basis or as an adjunct to your antiques or collectibles business. There is an increasing need for good appraisers in the insurance, business, and legal worlds; and appraisers are usually well paid.

The customary and most proper forms of payment are by the hour, day, or assignment. Fees range so broadly (anywhere from $25 to $250 per hour, as an example) across the board and are so dependent on local circumstances that you can best ascertain the going rate by speaking to other appraisers in your area.

There are, however, certain general guidelines. You should work pursuant to a written agreement setting forth the nature of the assignment, its purpose (insurance evaluation, et cetera), and the rate of compensation. In most cases, compensation should include time spent on research and writing up the report. Also, your expenses should be reimbursed upon proper documentation. However, though some appraisers insist upon it, I feel that the client should not pay for travel time to and from the job.

There are other forms of reimbursement employed by appraisers, especially those operating in fields other than antiques and collectibles. One is to key the fee to a percentage of the total appraised value of the property in question. The conflict of interest thus presented is so obvious as to make one wonder why any client would agree to it. A second method, sometimes employed in estate evaluations, is to base the fee on a percentage of the "tax savings" realized by the client through the appraiser's efforts. It is hard to imagine a greater inducement to fraud. Needless to say, the major associations of appraisers reject both systems.

Another limitation on your activity as an appraiser has to do with the question of buying what one evaluates. The general rule is "no." Any appraiser who offers, or agrees, to buy something that he or she has just appraised or is about to appraise casts doubt on his own integrity and that of his profession. The ability to be objective in the face of opportunity for profit may exist, but the public will not believe in it. Like Caesar's wife, the appraiser must be above suspicion. Keep your appraising business separate from your retail business, and you will make both businesses profitable.

20.

RESEARCH

Often the most successful dealers are also the most knowledgeable. By knowing as much as you can, not only about your own specialized field or fields of interest but also about antiques and collectibles in general, you obtain a substantial advantage over most of the competition.

Learning about your field is not really very different from acquiring a fund of information about any area of endeavor. It is a simple combination of experience and research. The former is both general and specific in nature, while the latter is often focused narrowly on a particular question or object.

Field Experience

What I choose to call "field experience" is really the heart and soul of the antiquer's professional life. Every time you go to or do a show, every time you attend a preview and an auction, visit a dealer's shop, look at a museum exhibition, or just sit and chew the fat with a bunch of people in the field, you are, or should be, acquiring knowledge and experience.

The well-rounded dealer does not confine his or her experience solely to the area in which he or she deals. Even though you may handle only fine clocks and watches, it is important that you have at least a smattering of knowledge in fields as diverse as Polynesian art and 1950s plastics.

This broad background is necessitated by the nature of today's antiques and collectibles market. First, ours is a national and even international market. With the mobility that most Americans possess, antiques originating in one area of the country are likely to show up in another one far away. A French *animalier* bronze that turns up in North Dakota may not be recognized by most of the local dealers and will probably bring far less than it would in New York or Los Angeles. An uncommon piece of North Carolina Moravian redware pottery might pass unnoticed at an antiques show in San Diego (where, in fact, I bought one at a fraction of its true value!).

The dealer who has enough general knowledge that the odd or unusual "rings a bell" is the one most likely to get the bargains. This is particularly important since quality antiques and collectibles are in greater demand than ever and are being sought by a growing legion of merchants. When you were one of a half-dozen dealers in a metropolitan region of some three hundred thousand inhabitants, there was a lot of merchandise to go around and you could afford to overlook things. Now there are two dozen dealers in that same area, and competition for the more popular and recognizable objects is fierce. The way to get an edge is to be able to recognize the uncommon.

The knowledge that allows you to do this is acquired over a period of time and from diverse sources. Visiting shows and attending auctions gives you a feel for what is popular and what it is bringing in the market. Let's say you see a crude planter made of unpeeled limbs and branches offered for five dollars at a house sale. You don't like it. It looks ill-made and boring. But if you'd gone to enough shows and seen these Adirondack pieces selling for sixty-five to eighty-five dollars, you would recognize a good buy.

Witnessing an auction bidding battle over a porcelain-headed Bru doll will soon convince you that not all "china head" dolls are created equal and that the maker's mark on a piece can raise the value dramatically. Clearly, one should be able at least to identify the more common French and German dolls.

Yet if you engage dealers and auctioneers in conversation, you will frequently learn that many of them handling these pieces do not know that much about them. They are often just relying on general gossip about "what's hot." For real information, turn to the specialist dealers and collectors. Some of these are reluctant to share their knowledge, but a promise to let them get first chance at something in their field of interest will often open the gates.

Cultivate museum curators and others who show an inclination for research. Museum personnel are or should be "above the battle" of the marketplace and can often provide important facts about an item's history and manufacture. Don't ask them about prices, though. It would be unethical for them to evaluate things.

Even if you can't find a museum director to befriend, attend all the exhibitions that are in any way related to the antiques and collectibles field. They will often give you a broader feel for an area which heretofore you knew only through one or two items, and in most cases the information you glean will be more complete and more accurate than you could hope to obtain from a dealer or auctioneer.

Research Materials

Whatever your experience, you will ultimately have to supplement what you pick up in the field with your own research.

It is here that many dealers miss the boat. They are content to operate on the basis of whatever knowledge they have absorbed through observation and conversation, yet often the most important questions can be answered only by going to the books.

Anyone who expects to be taken seriously in the antiques field should have a basic research library. The materials in your library will fall into three categories: general reference books; specialized studies; and periodicals, including auction catalogs.

Well-written general references such as Hazel Harrison's *World Antiques*, Arthur Chu's *Oriental Antiques and Collectibles*, and Helen Comstock's *Concise Encyclopedia of American Antiques* provide a clue to almost every puzzle, even though they often do not answer a specific question. These works also contain bibliographies of texts that deal more closely with specific areas.

Books on specialized studies focus more narrowly on a particular field, such as silver, furniture, or ceramics, or on a style category such as folk art or Art Nouveau. At a minimum, you should have every good book dealing with your own area of particular interest—for example, every available book on quilts if you collect or sell them. Beyond this, you may find yourself acquiring specialized texts in related fields. The quilt dealer or collector might, for example, find it necessary to have books on other textiles, such as coverlets, hooked rugs, and samplers.

Specialized studies should answer, at least in part, most of the questions you need answered. For exhaustive information or clues to something really obscure, you have to move into the area of research in original materials: business directories, census records, old newspapers, and the like. This process is too time-consuming and complex to be of much interest to most antiques and collectibles dealers.

The third class of reference materials includes magazines devoted to antiques and collectibles, newspaper-type weekly or monthly tabloids, and auction catalogs. The best magazines are *Connoisseur* and *The Magazine Antiques*. Both can be pretentious, and many articles are of interest only to decorators (such as the tedious photo stories of mansions stuffed with antebellum antiques) or graduate students in the decorative arts, but when these magazines cover a subject, they do it thoroughly and generally quite accurately.

The tabloids may occasionally provide some solid information, but the major contribution they offer is coverage of auctions and antiques shows. They give you up-to-date information on what is selling and what it is selling for.

Auction catalogs, such as those issued by Sotheby's, Christie's, and various regional auction houses, provide similar information, with the addition, in many cases, of extremely fine photography. Two caveats here: the information provided about the pieces to be sold is often erroneous, and the catalogs are sometimes more expensive than a good book on the subject. It is frequently possible, though, to find these catalogs remaindered in chain bookstores for a dollar or so apiece.

With the library described above you should be able to deal with all but the most obscure questions. You need only one more thing: the desire and curiosity to do the research. As a spur to your initiative, I offer "Ketchum's Law": "If you don't know what it is, it's probably valuable."

Every dealer has a series of tales about great finds made in the shops of other dealers—things he or she recognized and the other fellow didn't. Few are frank enough to admit the number of items they have "butched something off" (a dealers' term for selling an item you don't want or understand for a quick, low profit) because they didn't care to take the time and make the effort to figure out what the object was and what it was worth.

Cultivate an eye for the unusual and an ability to spot things that may have value. Don't expect to be able immediately to identify most of these objects. Few of us have the ability to retain enough information to do that. What you *can* strive for, though, is an intuition, based on broad general knowledge, that will prompt you to buy something or leave a deposit on it while you run home to do your research. Once you have made your first "killing" through this sort of study, you will probably be a lifelong student of your antiques and collectibles library! You will also be well on your way, not only to making a living in the business, but to flourishing in it.

And flourish you should hope to do if you will combine the three key elements, enthusiasm, knowledge, and integrity, to build your own antiques or collectibles business.

CALENDAR OF AMERICAN AND CANADIAN ANTIQUES SHOWS

This calendar is designed to provide the reader with a month-by-month listing of antiques and collectibles expositions selected from the many thousands held each year throughout the United States and Canada. Among the choices are major shows, good regional ones, and a substantial number of modest local expositions. The shows are listed by month, as specific show days vary each year, and within each month shows are listed alphabetically by state.

By using this listing in conjunction with Appendix II, "List of Antiques-Show Managers," dealers and would-be exhibitors should be able to locate expositions they might care to attend or take part in and to contact the managers for further information. (Where the management is not given, the show is run by a group of dealers.) Bear in mind also that show dates and managements change rapidly, and some of this information will, of necessity, be obsolete within a few months or years.

January

Dothan, Alabama. Wiregrass Commons Mall Antiques Show. Mary Jo Collier

Scottsdale, Arizona. Safari Inn Resort Antiques Show. Southwest Antiques Guild

Glendale, California. The All-American Collector's Show. All-American Management

Denver, Colorado. Collectors' Extravaganza. Walt and Nancy Johnson

Wilton, Connecticut. Fatima Antiques Festival. Success Promotions

Washington, D.C. Washington Antiques Show. Arthur Jackson

Pompano Beach, Florida. Coral Springs Philharmonic Society Antiques Show. Zita Waters Bell

Savannah, Georgia. Historic Savannah Antiques Show. Bud Maron

Peoria, Illinois. Mid-America Antiques Show. Mid-America Management

Bloomington, Indiana. Bloomington Antiques Show. G & G Promotions

Topeka, Kansas. International Antique Show. International Shows Management

Burlington, Kentucky. Burlington Antiques Show. Paul Kohls

Brunswick, Maine. Brunswick Armory Show.

Annapolis, Maryland. Annapolis Heritage Antiques Show. Peggy Stewart Antiques Shows

Boston, Massachusetts. Copley Plaza Hotel Antiques Show. Sonia Paine Management

Kalamazoo, Michigan. Antique Dealers' Wholesale Market. Dayna Alexander Productions

Hattiesburg, Mississippi. Cloverleaf Mall Antiques Show. Jack Hatfield

Kansas City, Missouri. World Wide Antiques Show. World Wide Antiques Show Productions

Hampton Falls, New Hampshire. The Greenhouse Antiques Show. Coastal Promotions, Inc.

Morristown, New Jersey. Morristown Antiques Show. Diane
    Wendy
New York City, New York. Winter Antiques Show. N. Pen-
    dergast Jones
Syracuse, New York. Salt City Winter Antiques Show. Andrew
    Hengst
Springfield, Ohio. Springfield Antiques Show and Flea Mar-
    ket. Bruce and Shari Knight
Oklahoma City, Oklahoma. Antique Show. Continental
    Shows, Ltd.
N. Pickering, Ontario, Canada. Durham Antiques Market.
    George Gouldburn
New Hope, Pennsylvania. New Hope Winter Antiques Show.
    David and Peter Mancuso
Charleston, South Carolina. Gaillard Auditorium Antiques
    Show. Chapman Shows, Inc.
Knoxville, Tennessee. Esau's Antiques and Collectibles Mar-
    ket. Esau's Management
Fort Worth, Texas. International Show. International Shows
    Management
Woodstock, Vermont. Woodstock Inn Antiques Show. Mar-
    jorie Barry
Richmond, Virginia. Richmond Antiques Show. Bellman Pro-
    ductions
Cedarburg, Wisconsin. Cure for Cabin Fever Antiques Show.

February

Tuscaloosa, Alabama. Antiques Show. Mary Jo Collier
Phoenix, Arizona. Phoenix Antiques Show. Acorn Antique
    Guild
Pasadena, California. Pasadena Antiques Market. Caskey-
    Lees
Norwalk, Connecticut. Norwalk Armory Antiques Show. Jus-
    tinius Management

Miami, Florida. D. S. Clarke Miami Antique Show. Maron Management

Atlanta, Georgia. Atlanta Antiques Extravaganza. Anthony Gergely

Grayslake, Illinois. Grayslake Antiques and Collectibles Show. Lake County Promotions

South Bend, Indiana. Antique Dealers' Market. Ark Productions

Salina, Kansas. Antiques Show. Exploring Antiques Shows

Louisville, Kentucky. Kentuckian Mid-Winter Antiques Market. Rod Lich

Baton Rouge, Louisiana. Antiques Show. Glad-Mor Productions

Baltimore, Maryland. Maryland Antiques Show. Arthur Jackson

Kalamazoo, Michigan. Antique Dealers' Wholesale Market. Dayna Alexander Promotions

Chestnut Hill, Massachusetts. The Brimmer and May School Antiques Show. Circa Management

Columbus, Mississippi. Antique Show. Mary Jo Collier

Kalispell, Montana. Great Northwest Antiques and Coin Show. John Copenhaver

Omaha, Nebraska. International Antiques Show. International Shows Management

Concord, New Hampshire. Concord Antiques Fair. S. K. French

Lawrenceville, New Jersey. Lawrenceville/Mercer County Antiques Show. David and Peter Mancuso

Albuquerque, New Mexico. Convention Center Antiques Show. Continental Shows, Ltd.

White Plains, New York. White Plains Antiques Show. Diane Wendy

Columbus, Ohio. Columbus Antiques Flea Market. Stockwell Promotions

Tulsa, Oklahoma. World Wide Antiques Show. World Wide
Antiques Shows Productions
Philadelphia, Pennsylvania. Pennsylvania's Finest Antiques
Show. Bellman Productions
Greenville, South Carolina. Antiques Show. Jack Hatfield
Nashville, Tennessee. Heart of Country Antiques Show.
Richard E. Kramer Management
Dallas, Texas. The Tri Delta Charity Antiques Show. Tri Delta
Alumni Show Management
Woodstock, Vermont. Cabin Fever Antiques Show. Bob and
Mary Fraser
Richmond, Virginia. Science Museum of Virginia Antiques
Show. O'Bannon Shows
Seattle, Washington. America's Largest Antiques and Collect-
ibles Sales. Don Wirfs and Associates
Wausau Center, Wisconsin. Wausau Center Antiques Show.
Ray Hanson

March

Phoenix, Arizona. Antiques Market. Arthur Schwartz
Santa Rosa, California. B & H Antiques Show. Robert
Fulkerson
Fort Collins, Colorado. Fort Collins Antiques Show. Exploring
Antiques Shows
New Haven, Connecticut. New Haven Antiques Show. Milton
and Robert Cottler
Washington, D.C. National Capital Antiques Show. Diane
Wendy
Naples, Florida. Naples Antiques Show. Peggy Stewart An-
tiques Shows
Atlanta, Georgia. Atlanta Antiques Show. Bud and Muriel
Maron
Winnetka, Illinois. Winnetka Antiques Show. Rebecca Murray

Indianapolis, Indiana. Hoosier Antiques Exposition. Ronald Cox

Iowa City, Iowa. Iowa City Spring Antiques Show. Hanson Promotions

Overland Park, Kansas. Wagner Promotions Antiques Show. Wagner Promotions, Inc.

Louisville, Kentucky. The Collegiate School Antiques Show. N. Pendergast Jones

Augusta, Maine. The Augusta Civic Center Spring Antiques Show. Coastal Promotions, Inc.

Woburn, Massachusetts. Northeast Collectibles Extravaganza. Show Promotion

Dearborn, Michigan. Great Lakes Antiques Show. Nordell Management

Shakopee, Minnesota. Minnesota National Antiques Exposition. Zurko's Midwest Promotions

Tupelo, Mississippi. Natchez Trace Convention Center Antiques Show. Bagwell Antique Shows

Joplin, Missouri. International Antiques Show. International Shows Management

Holdredge, Nebraska. Antiques Show. Exploring Antiques Shows

Las Vegas, Nevada. Cashman Center Antiques Show. Sy Miller Productions

Nashua, New Hampshire. St. Stan's Hall Antiques Show. Jack Donigian

Atlantic City, New Jersey. Atlantique City Antiques Show. Norman Schaut

New York City, New York. The Spring Pier Antiques Show and Tribal Arts Show. McHugh Presentations

Columbus, Ohio. Antiques Market. Vintage Promotions

Oklahoma City, Oklahoma. Antiques Show. International Shows Management

Bowmanville, Ontario, Canada. Bowmanville Antiques Show.

Portland, Oregon. America's Largest Antiques and Collectibles Sale. Don Wirfs & Associates

New Hope, Pennsylvania. Bucks County Antiques Show. David and Peter Mancuso

Providence, Rhode Island. The Rhode Island Antiques Show. Jacqueline Sideli

Myrtle Beach, South Carolina. Antiques Show. Chapman Shows, Inc.

Maryville, Tennessee. Foothills Mall Antiques Show. Mary Jo Collier

Wallis, Texas. Spring Antiques Show. Savell and Schluter

Salt Lake City, Utah. Antiques Show. Walter Larsen and Associates

Woodstock, Vermont. Antiques Show. Marjorie Barry

Richmond, Virginia. Richmond Antiques Festival. Bellman Productions

Yakima, Washington. Masonic Center Antiques Show. Walter Larsen and Associates

Appleton, Wisconsin. Valley Antiques Show. Zurko's Midwest Promotions

April

Tuscaloosa, Alabama. Tuscaloosa Antiques Show. Town and Country Antiques Management

Scottsdale, Arizona. Scottsdale Antiques Show. Acorn Antique Guild

Pasadena, California. Nostalgia Collectibles Show and Sale. Doug Wright Productions

Grand Junction, Colorado. Grand Junction Antiques Show. Exploring Antiques Shows

Hartford, Connecticut. Connecticut Spring Antiques Show. Forbes and Turner

Wilmington, Delaware. Wilmington Antiques Show. Barry Schlecker

Jacksonville, Florida. Jacksonville Antiques Show. KJR Joint Venture

Chamblee, Georgia. Chamblee Spring Antiques Festival. Shirley Maddox

Rosemont, Illinois. Chicago O'Hare Spring Antiques Show. Shador/Manor House

Indianapolis, Indiana. Methodist Hospital Antiques Show. Dolphin Promotions

Cedar Rapids, Iowa. Cedar Rapids Antiques Show and Collectors' Fair. Donald C. Koehn

Overland Park, Kansas. Spofford Antiques Show and Sale. Elva Needles

Lexington, Kentucky. Horseman's Antiques Show and Sale. MO Productions

Lafayette, Louisiana. Acadania Mall Antiques Show. Jack Hatfield

Brunswick, Maine. The Brunswick Armory Antiques Show. Brunswick Armory Show Management

Gaithersburg, Maryland. D.C. Area Winter Antiques Market. Bellman Productions

West Springfield, Massachusetts. The Eastern States Antiques and Collectibles Show. The Maven Company

Ann Arbor, Michigan. Ann Arbor Antiques Market. Margaret Brusher

Owatonna, Minnesota. Antiques Show. Chase Antique Shows

Biloxi, Mississippi. Coast Coliseum Antiques Show. Town and Country Antiques Management

Kansas City, Missouri. Gillis Antiques Show Extravaganza. Fine Americana Shows

Hastings, Nebraska. Antiques Show. Exploring Antiques Shows

Amherst, New Hampshire. Amherst Outdoor Antiques Market. Carlson Management

Morristown, New Jersey. Morristown Antiques Show. Diane Wendy

Albuquerque, New Mexico. Antiques Show. Continental
Shows, Ltd.
Albany, New York. The Albany Armory Antiques Show.
Jacqueline Sideli
Winston-Salem, North Carolina. Winston-Salem Antiques
Show. Arthur Jackson
Grand Forks, North Dakota. Grand Forks Antiques Show.
Midwest Antique Guild
Columbus, Ohio. Columbus Antiques Flea Market. Stockwell
Promotions
Philadelphia, Pennsylvania. Philadelphia Hospital Show. Rus-
sell Carrell
Montreal, Quebec, Canada. Jacques-Cartier Antiques Flea
Market.
Providence, Rhode Island. The Rhode Island Antiques Show.
Jacqueline Sideli
Spartanburg, South Carolina. Antiques Show. Lambeth's
Management
Lebanon, Tennessee. Middle Tennessee Antiques Market.
MO Productions
Round Top, Texas. Antiques Show. Antiques Productions
Woodstock, Vermont. Antiques Show. Marjorie Barry
Charlottesville, Virginia. Charlottesville Spring Antiques
Show. Zita Waters Bell
Kirkland, Washington. Antiques Exposition. Western An-
tiques Expositions
Wheeling, West Virginia. Antiques Show. Jim Reynolds
Milwaukee, Wisconsin. Milwaukee/National Antiques Expo-
sition. Zurko's Midwest Promotions

May

Phoenix, Arizona. Antiques Market. Arthur Schwartz
Santa Monica, California. The L.A. Show—Modernism.
Richard Wordell

Aurora, Colorado. Antiques Show. World Wide Antiques
Shows Productions
Woodbridge, Connecticut. Woodbridge Antiques Festival.
Forbes and Turner
Sarasota, Florida. Americana Antiques Show. August Antiques
Management
Atlanta, Georgia. Atlanta Antiques Show. Bud and Muriel
Maron
Deerfield, Illinois. Trinity Springs Antiques Festival. Zurko's
Midwest Promotions
Lawrenceburg, Indiana. Tri-State Antiques Market. MO Pro-
ductions
Burlington, Kentucky. Burlington Antiques Show. Paul Kohls
Kennebunk, Maine. Antiques Show. Lillyann H. Rowe
Baltimore and Columbia, Maryland. "East" and "West" Side
Antiques Shows. Bellman Productions
Brimfield, Massachusetts. Brimfield Antiques Markets.
Richard May, J.A. "Jake" Mathieu
Dearborn, Michigan. Greenfield Village Antiques Show.
J. Jordan Humberstone
Rochester, Minnesota. Antiques Show. Chase Antique Shows
St. Louis, Missouri. St. Louis Antiques Show. N. Pendergast
Jones
Keene, New Hampshire. Antiques/Collectibles Show and
Sale. O'Brien Enterprises
Stanhope, New Jersey. Waterloo Village Antiques Fair. Stella
Show Management
Rhinebeck, New York. Rhinebeck Antiques Fair. Bill Walters
Shows, Inc.
Durham, North Carolina. The Durham Antiques Show and
Sale. Zita Waters Bell
Chagrin Falls, Ohio. Chagrin Falls Antiques Show. Ted
Kromer
Oklahoma City, Oklahoma. Antique Show. Jeanne Fishman
Ontario, Canada. St. Jacobs Country Antiques Show.

Chadds Ford, Pennsylvania. Brandywine River Museum Antiques Show. Peggy Stewart Antiques Shows

Westerly, Rhode Island. Antiques Show. Country Cape Antiques Shows

Columbia, South Carolina. Antiques Show. The Nelson Garretts, Inc.

Sioux Falls, South Dakota. Coliseum Antiques Show. Midwest Antique Guild

Knoxville, Tennessee. Antiques and Collectibles Market. Esau's Management

Houston, Texas. Houston Proud Antiques Show. Savell and Schluter

Woodstock, Vermont. Antiques Show. Marjorie Barry

Alexandria, Virginia. Antiques Show. Evelyn Sturza

Ocean Shores, Washington. Antiques Show. JP Promotions

Wauwatosa, Wisconsin. Antiques Show. Glad-Mor Productions

June

Flagstaff, Arizona. Flagstaff Antiques Show. Acorn Antique Guild

Glendale, California. Great Collectibles Show and Sale. Doug Wright Productions

Durango, Colorado. Antiques Show. Continental Shows, Ltd.

Farmington, Connecticut. Farmington Antiques Weekend. Don Mackey

Washington, D.C. Antiques-on-the-Potomac. McHugh Presentations

Mt. Dora, Florida. Antiques Fair. Florida Twin Markets Management

Gainesville, Georgia. Georgia Mountains Center Antiques Show. KJR Joint Venture Shows

Lake Forest, Illinois. Lake Forest College Antiques Show. Zurko's Midwest Promotions

Indianapolis, Indiana. Summer Antique Advertising Show.
L-W Promotions

Wichita, Kansas. Antiques Show. International Shows Management

Louisville, Kentucky. Kentuckiana Summer Sunday. Rod Lich

Cumberland, Maine. Americana Celebration Antiques Show.
Nan Gurley

Gaithersburg, Maryland. Antique Dolls, Toys, and Games
Show. Bellman Productions

Topsfield, Massachusetts. Great Indoor-Outdoor Antiques
Show. Drummer Boys Management

Saginaw, Michigan. Michigan Antiques Festival. Michigan
Antiques Festival Management

Biloxi, Mississippi. Antiques Show. Jack Hatfield

Springfield, Missouri. Antiques Show. Southwest MO's

Reno, Nevada. Reno-Sparks Antiques Show. Bustamente Enterprises, Inc.

Keene, New Hampshire. Antiques/Collectibles Show and
Sale. O'Brien Enterprises

Jersey City, New Jersey. Liberty Collectibles Exposition.
Stella Show Management Company

Albuquerque, New Mexico. Antiques Show. Continental
Shows, Ltd.

Round Lake, New York. Round Lake Antiques Festival. Emily
Smith Shows

Rocky Mount, North Carolina. Antiques Fair. Mary Jo Collier

Cincinnati, Ohio. Greater Cincinnati Antiques Show. Ronald
Cox

Tulsa, Oklahoma. Antiques Show. International Shows Management

Christie Park, Ontario, Canada. Carlisle Classic Antiques
Show.

Erwinna, Pennsylvania. Tinicum Park Antiques Show. Katona
and Lutz

Middletown, Rhode Island. Aquidneck Island Antiques Show. Florence Archambault

Myrtle Beach, South Carolina. Antiques Show. Chapman Shows, Inc.

Lebanon, Tennessee. Middle Tennessee Antiques Market. MO Productions

Austin, Texas. Gulf Coast Antiques Show. Gulf Coast Antiques Shows

Weathersfield Center, Vermont. Weathersfield Meeting House Antiques Show.

Lynchburg, Virginia. Antiques Show. D'Amore Productions

Tacoma, Washington. America's Largest Antiques and Collectibles Sales. Don Wirfs and Associates

Lewisburg, West Virginia. Antiques Show.

Elkhorn, Wisconsin. Walworth County Fairgrounds Antiques Show. Promotions

Casper, Wyoming. Antiques Show. Casper Antique and Collectors Club

July

Beverly Hills, California. Beverly Hills Antiques Show. Bud and Muriel Maron

Gunnison, Colorado. Antiques Show. World Wide Antiques Shows Productions

Guilford, Connecticut. Guilford Keeping Society Antiques Festival. Merle L. Hornstein

Melbourne, Florida. Eau Gallie Civic Center Antiques and Collectibles Show. Bill Arflin

Marietta, Georgia. Antiques Show. KJR Joint Venture

Arlington Heights, Illinois. Antiques Show. Zurko's Midwest Promotions

Lawrenceburg, Indiana. Tri-State Antiques Market. MO Productions

Solon, Iowa. Open Air Antiques Show. Hanson Promotions

Wichita, Kansas. Antiques Show. Continental Shows, Ltd.

Burlington, Kentucky. Burlington Antiques Show. Paul Kohls

Kennebunk, Maine. Kennebunk Antiques Show. James Montell

Baltimore, Maryland. Antiques Show. Town and Country Antiques Management

Sudbury, Massachusetts. Sudbury Antiques Show. Nan Gurley

Adrian, Michigan. Adrian Antiques Market. Claudette and Grant Swift

Lafayette, Mississippi. Antiques Show. Bagwell Antique Shows

Grand Island, Nebraska. Antiques Show. Exploring Antiques Shows

Wolfboro, New Hampshire. Wolfboro Antiques Show. E.M.C. French

Cape May, New Jersey. Cold Spring Village Antiques Show. Stella Show Management

Santa Fe, New Mexico. Antiques Show. Continental Shows, Ltd.

Sodus, New York. Sodus Shaker Heritage Antiques Show. S. Kline

Franklin, North Carolina. Antiques Show. KJR Joint Venture

Richfield, Ohio. Pappabello Coliseum Antiques Show. June Greenwald

Perth, Ontario, Canada. Perth Antiques Show. Country Lane Management

Portland, Oregon. America's Largest Antiques and Collectibles Sales. Don Wirfs and Associates

Ephrata, Pennsylvania. Historic Ephrata Antiques Show. Paul Ettline

North Hatley, Quebec, Canada. North Hatley Antiques Show.

Myrtle Beach, South Carolina. Antiques Show. Chapman Shows, Inc.

Nashville, Tennessee. Antiques Show. G & G Promotions
Austin, Texas. Austin Antiques Show. Emma Lee Turney
Dorset, Vermont. Dorset Antiques Festival. Forbes and
    Turner
Falls Church, Virginia. Antiques Show. Evelyn Sturza
Fish Creek, Wisconsin. Door County Antiques Show.
    Burkhardt-Laughlin Management

August

Huntsville, Alabama. Antiques Show. Mary Jo Collier
Prescott, Arizona. Prescott Antiques Show. Acorn Antique
    Guild
Long Beach, California. Outdoor Antiques and Collectibles
    Market. Americana Enterprises
Aurora, Colorado. Antiques Show. World Wide Antiques
    Shows Productions
Madison, Connecticut. Exchange Club of Madison Antiques
    Show. David Schafer
Melbourne, Florida. Antiques and Collectibles Show. Bill
    Arflin
Augusta, Georgia. Antiques Show and Craft Market. Boutwell
    Promotions
Rockford, Illinois. Rockford/National Mid-Summer Antiques
    Fair. Zurko's Midwest Promotions
Marion, Indiana. Antiques Show. G & G Promotions
Topeka, Kansas. Expocentre Antiques Show. International
    Shows Management
Burlington, Kentucky. Burlington Antiques Show. Paul Kohls
Kennebunk, Maine. Antiques Show. Goosefare Promotions
Hyattsville, Maryland. Prince George's Plaza Antiques Show.
    Heirloom Promotions
Orleans, Massachusetts. Cape Cod Antiques Exposition. Com-
    pass Antiques Shows

Centreville, Michigan. The Affordable Antiques Market. J. Jordan Humberstone

Duluth, Minnesota. Arena Antiques Show. Midwest Antique Guild

Reno, Nevada. Antiques and Collectibles Show. Don Wirfs and Associates

Wolfeboro, New Hampshire. Wolfeboro Antiques Fair and Sale. E.M.C. French

Annandale, New Jersey. Antiques in August. Don and Joyce Coffman

Santa Fe, New Mexico. American Indian Art Show and Sale. Don Bennett and Associates

Bouckville, New York. Madison-Bouckville Antiques Show. Andrew Hengst

Fayetteville, North Carolina. Cross Creek Antiques Show. Heirloom Promotions

Cincinnati, Ohio. Indian Hill Antiques Fair. Mongenas

Oklahoma City, Oklahoma. Antiques Show. International Shows Management

Odessa, Ontario, Canada. Odessa Antiques Show. Dobson and Girling

Meadowland, Pennsylvania. Antiques Fair at the Meadows. The Old Show

Newport, Rhode Island. Newport Yachting Center Antiques Show. Bob Fricker and Son

Myrtle Beach, South Carolina. Antiques Show. Chapman Shows, Inc.

Knoxville, Tennessee. Antiques and Collectibles Market. Esau's Management

Houston, Texas. Houston Antiques Show. Emma Lee Turney

Stratton, Vermont. Vermont Antiques Dealers Association Antiques Show. Warren Kimble

Fredricksburg, Virginia. Spotsylvania Antiques Show. Heirloom Promotions

Ocean Shores, Washington. Antiques Show. JP Promotions

Elkhorn, Wisconsin. Walworth County Fairgrounds Antiques Market. G & G Promotions

September

Montgomery, Alabama. Antiques Show. Mary Jo Collier

Mesa, Arizona. Mesa Antiques Show. Acorn Antique Guild

Glendale, California. Great Collectibles Show and Sale. Doug Wright Productions

New Haven, Connecticut. Fall New Haven Antiques Show. Milton and Robert Cottler

Newark, Delaware. Antiques Show. Evelyn Sturza

Washington, D.C. Mount Vernon College Antiques Show. Town and Country Antiques Management

Lake Worth, Florida. Lake Worth Antiques Festival. A & W Productions, Inc.

Columbus, Georgia. Columbus Square Antiques Show. Heirloom Promotions

Pecatonica, Illinois. The "Pec Thing" Antiques Fair. ABC Productions

Indianapolis, Indiana. Home in Indiana Antiques Show. Richard E. Kramer Management

DesMoines, Iowa. Merle Hay Antiques Show. Pat Combs Promotions

Wichita, Kansas. Antiques Show. World Wide Antiques Shows

Burlington, Kentucky. Burlington Antiques Show. Paul Kohls

South Portland, Maine. Portland Symphony Orchestra Antiques Show. Forbes and Turner

Baltimore, Maryland. Baltimore Summer Antiques Fair. Shador/Manor House

Sandwich, Massachusetts. The Heritage Plantation Antiques Show. Jacqueline Sideli

Birmingham, Michigan. Birmingham Methodist Antiques Show. Willmann's Shows

Minneapolis, Minnesota. Minneapolis Institute of Arts Antiques Show. M.I.A. Antiques Show

Rochester, Minnesota. Apache Mall Antiques Show. Chase
Antique Shows
Joplin, Missouri. Joplin Antiques Show. International Shows
Management
Kalispell, Montana. Great Northwest Antiques and Coin
Show. John Copenhaver
Grand Island, Nebraska. Antiques Show. Exploring Antiques
Shows
Amherst, New Hampshire. Amherst Outdoor Antiques Mar-
ket. Carlson Management
Stanhope, New Jersey. Waterloo Village Antiques Fair. Stella
Show Management
Santa Fe, New Mexico. Antiques Show. Continental Shows,
Ltd.
New York, New York. The International Antique Dealers
Show. Brian and Anna Haughton
Stormville, New York. Stormville Airport Antiques Show and
Flea Market. Pat Carnahan
Charlotte, North Carolina. Carolina Country Antiques Show.
Betty Williams
Columbus, Ohio. Greater Columbus Antiques Show. M & M
Enterprises
Aberfoyle, Ontario, Canada. Flamboro Antiques Show. Flam-
boro Management
Kingston, Ontario, Canada. Nepean Sports Complex Antiques
Show. Scott Promotions
St. George, Ontario, Canada. St. George Antiques Fair and
Sale. St. George Management
Greensburg, Pennsylvania. Greensburg Antiques Show. Ruth
and Dale Van Kuren
Myrtle Beach, South Carolina. Antiques Show. Chapman
Shows, Inc.
Sioux Falls, South Dakota. Antiques Show. Midwest Antique
Guild

Chattanooga, Tennessee. Northgate Mall Antiques Show. Jack
   Hatfield
Houston, Texas. Theta Charity Antiques Show. Zita Waters
   Bell
Woodstock, Vermont. Woodstock Antiques Show. Stephen R.
   Allman
Richmond, Virginia. The Richmond Antiques and Flea Mar-
   ket. Heritage Productions
Milwaukee, Wisconsin. Milwaukee County Historical Society
   Antiques Show. Milwaukee County Historical Society

October

Yuma, Arizona. Yuma Antiques Show. Acorn Antique Guild
San Francisco, California. San Francisco Fall Antiques Show.
   Russell Carrell
Denver, Colorado. Merchandise Mart Antiques Show. World
   Wide Antiques Shows
Trumbull, Connecticut. Trumbull Historical Society Antiques
   Show and Sale. Louise Jacques
Washington, D.C. D.C. Fall Antiques Fair. Shador/Manor
   House
Miami Beach, Florida. Winter Miami Beach Antiques Show.
   Grover and Baron
Atlanta, Georgia. The Fall Atlanta Antiques Show. Bud and
   Muriel Maron
Chicago, Illinois. Chicago International Antiques Show. The
   Lakeside Group
Fort Wayne, Indiana. Fort Wayne Antiques Show and Sale.
   Ray Goldsberry
Cedar Rapids, Iowa. Midwest Antiques Market. Paula Van
   Deest
Overland Park, Kansas. Metcalf Mall Antiques Show. Jeanne
   Fishman

Owensboro, Kentucky. Town Square Antiques Show. G & G
Promotions
Portland, Maine. Maine Fall Antiques Exposition. Goosefare
Promotions
Columbia, Maryland. Mid-Atlantic Antiques Market. Sims
Rogers
Hancock, Massachusetts. The Hancock Shaker Village An-
tiques Show. Jacqueline Sideli
Kalamazoo, Michigan. Maple Hill Antiques Show. Gloria
Seigert
Shakopee, Minnesota. Canterbury Downs Antiques Show.
Zurko's Midwest Promotions
Labradie, Missouri. County Harvest Antiques Festival. Vanita
Zehule
Omaha, Nebraska. Convention Center Antiques Show. In-
ternational Shows Management
Nashua, New Hampshire. Nashua Antiques Show. Jack Doni-
gian
Cape May, New Jersey. Antiques in Congress Hall. Don and
Joyce Coffman
New York City, New York. The Fall Antiques Show at the Pier.
Sanford L. Smith and Associates
Charlotte, North Carolina. Min & Museum Antiques Show.
Min & Museum Auxiliary
Cincinnati, Ohio. Greater Cincinnati Antiques Show. Ronald
Cox
Tulsa, Oklahoma. Antiques Show. Jeanne Fishman
Kingston, Ontario, Canada. Frontenac Antiques Show. Scott
Promotions
Portland, Oregon. Antiques Show. Don Wirfs and Associates
Pottstown, Pennsylvania. Great Pottstown Antiques Show.
Antiques Dealers Association of Montgomery County
East Providence, Rhode Island. Fall Antiques Show.
Charleston, South Carolina. Gaillard Auditorium Antiques
Show. The Nelson Garretts, Inc.

Chattanooga, Tennessee. The Houston Museum Antiques Show. The Houston Museum Committee

Austin, Texas. Austin Lyric Opera Fall Antiques Show. Lyric Management

Bullville, Texas. Bullville Antiques Festival. Frank Cheely

Weston, Vermont. Weston Antiques Show. Weston Antiques Show Management

Richmond, Virginia. Richmond Antiques Extravaganza. Antiques Extravaganzas, Inc.

Kirkland, Washington. Antiques Exposition. Western Antiques Expositions

Cedarburg, Wisconsin. Cedarburg Antiques Show. Trudy Hannam

November

Tuscaloosa, Alabama. University Mall Antiques Show. Mary Jo Collier

Scottsdale, Arizona. Antiques Show. Bustamente Enterprises, Inc.

North Little Rock, Arkansas. New Convention Center Antiques Show. International Shows Management

San Mateo, California. Hillsborough Antiques Show and Sale. United Voluntary Services

Denver, Colorado. Antiques Show. World Wide Antiques Shows

Norwalk, Connecticut. Remember November Antiques Show. Success Promotions

Washington, D.C. District of Columbia Antiques Show. Diane Wendy

Gainesville, Florida. Gainesville Woman's Club Antiques Show. KJR Joint Venture

Atlanta, Georgia. High Museum Antiques Show. Russell Carrell

St. Charles, Illinois. The Original Antiques Show. Easy Time Productions

Indianapolis, Indiana. Annual Antiques Spectacular. L-W Promotions

Davenport, Iowa. Wonderland Antiques Show. Dova Pitts

Overland Park, Kansas. Merchandise Mart Antiques Show. Wagner Promotions, Inc.

Hopkinsville, Kentucky. Antiques Show. G & G Promotions

New Orleans, Louisiana. Rivergate Exposition Center Antiques Show. Dolphin Promotions

Augusta, Maine. Augusta Armory Antiques Show. James Montell

Baltimore, Maryland. Baltimore Antiques Show. Town and Country Antiques Management

West Springfield, Massachusetts. The Eastern States Doll, Toy, and Teddy Bear Show. The Maven Company

Dearborn, Michigan. Great Lakes Antiques Show. Nordell Management

Minneapolis, Minnesota. Pure and Simple Antiques Show. Johnson and Moir Antique Shows

Jackson, Mississippi. Mississippi Trade Mart Antiques Show. Bagwell Antique Shows

Webster Groves, Missouri. Webster Groves Antiques Show. Frank Cheely

Nashua, New Hampshire. St. Stan's Hall Antiques Show. Jack Donigian

Ridgewood, New Jersey. College Club of Ridgewood Antiques Show. College Club Management

Albuquerque, New Mexico. Antiques Show. Continental Shows, Ltd.

Niagara Falls, New York. Niagara Falls International Antiques Show. Andrew Hengst

Winston-Salem, North Carolina. Winston-Salem Antiques Extravaganza. Antiques Extravaganzas, Inc.

Columbus, Ohio. Columbus Antiques Flea Market. Stockwell Promotions

Tulsa, Oklahoma. Antiques Show. International Shows Management
Toronto, Ontario, Canada. Toronto Antiques Show and Sale.
Jamison, Pennsylvania. Heart of Bucks Antiques Show. Bob Lutz
Spartanburg, South Carolina. Holiday Antiques Showcase. Galloway Promotions
Nashville, Tennessee. Nashville Flea Market. Salas Concessions
Kerrville, Texas. Christmas in the Hills Antiques Show. Titsworth Productions
Burlington, Vermont. Burlington Antiques Show. Marjorie Barry
Alexandria, Virginia. Historic Alexandria Antiques Show. Peggy Stewart Antiques Shows, Inc.
West Bend, Wisconsin. Silver Brook Holiday Market. Wiething Promotions

December

Palm Springs, California. Convention Center Antiques Show. Calendar Antique Shows
Old Greenwich, Connecticut. The Greenwich Antiques Market. Jacqueline Sideli
West Jacksonville, Florida. Jacksonville Christmas Show. Peggy Stewart Antiques Shows, Inc.
Atlanta, Georgia. Atlanta Antiques Extravaganza. Anthony Gergely
Grayslake, Illinois. Grayslake Antiques and Collectibles Show. Lake County Promotions
Indianapolis, Indiana. Hoosier Antiques Exposition. Ronald Cox
Burlington, Kentucky. Burlington Antiques Show. Paul Kohls

Gaithersburg, Maryland. Antique Dolls, Toys, and Games Show. Bellman Productions

Boston, Massachusetts. Northeast Collectibles Extravaganza. Show Promotion

Hudson, New Hampshire. Holt's Antique Doll Show. Holt's Antiques Shows

New York City, New York. The Collector's Eye Antiques Show. Edwin T. Palko

Springfield, Ohio. Springfield Antiques Show and Flea Market. Bruce and Shari Knight

Oklahoma City, Oklahoma. Fairgrounds Antiques Show. International Shows Management

Hamburg, Pennsylvania. Hamburg Antiques Market. Rosemary Schorr and Barry Dobinsky

Nashville, Tennessee. Nashville Flea Market. Salas Concessions

Wichita Falls, Texas. Antiques Show. Continental Shows, Ltd.

Woodstock, Vermont. Marjorie Barry's Antiques Show. Marjorie Barry

Milwaukee, Wisconsin. Brewery Collectibles Show. Jim Welytok

LIST OF

ANTIQUES-SHOW MANAGERS

Where no number is given for a manager, it is an indication that the manager does not take telephone inquiries.

A & W Productions, Inc.	305-561-5792
ABC Productions	815-239-1188
Acorn Antique Guild	602-962-5503
Alexander, Dayna Productions	616-344-2419
All-American Management	213-392-6676
Allman, Stephen R.	802-334-8894
Americana Enterprises	213-655-5703
Antiques Dealers Assoc. of Montgomery County	215-323-6122
Antiques Extravaganzas, Inc.	919-924-8337
Antiques Productions	713-520-8057
Archambault, Florence	401-846-9024
Arflin, Bill	305-777-3058
Ark Productions	800-234-2531
August Antiques Management	813-351-6666

Bagwell Antique Shows	601-939-1243
Barry, Marjorie	603-939-1243
Bell, Zita Waters	407-483-4047
Bellman Productions	301-329-2188
Bennett, Don & Associates	818-991-5596
Boutwell Promotions	404-724-8301
Brunswick Armory Show Management	207-832-5550
Brusher, Margaret	Ann Arbor, MI 48106
Burkhardt-Laughlin Management	414-743-9100
Bustamente Enterprises, Inc.	209-358-3134
Calendar Antique Shows	714-682-7980
Carlson Management	617-641-0600
Carnahan, Pat	914-221-6561
Carrell, Russell	Salisbury, CT 06068
Caskey-Lees	213-396-0876
Casper Antique and Collectors Club	307-234-6663
Chapman Shows, Inc.	704-625-9261
Chase Antique Shows	612-780-1309
Cheely, Frank	409-865-3264
Circa Management	508-651-3101
Coastal Promotions, Inc.	207-563-1013
Coffman, Don and Joyce	413-229-2433
College Club Management	201-444-4240
Collier, Mary Jo	404-662-6640
Combs, Pat, Promotions	913-441-3306
Compass Antiques Shows	617-749-0138
Continental Shows, Ltd.	806-622-0727
Copenhaver, John	406-257-8014
Cottler, Milton and Robert	203-387-7006
Country Cape Antiques Shows	401-377-8116
Country Lane Management	613-267-4686
Cox, Ronald	317-773-1131

D'Amore Productions	Virginia Beach, VA
Dobson and Girling	613-283-1168
Dolphin Promotions	305-563-6747
Donigian, Jack	617-329-1192
Drummer Boys Management	617-229-6480
Esau's Management	615-588-1233
Easy Time Productions	312-858-9631
Ettline, Paul	
Exploring Antiques Shows	303-226-0721
Fine Americana Shows	913-381-8610
Fishman, Jeanne	313-548-9066
Flamboro Management	416-685-1225
Florida Twin Markets Management	904-383-8393
Forbes and Turner Management	207-767-3967
Fraser, Bob and Mary	802-446-2463
French, E. M. C.	603-772-3359
French, S. K.	603-772-3359
Fricker, Bob and Son	508-336-6600
Fulkerson, Robert	415-276-0424
G & G Promotions	812-334-3354
Galloway Promotions	803-585-7912
Garretts, The Nelson, Inc.	803-884-7204
Gergely, Anthony	404-769-8129
Glad-Mor Productions	414-351-3039
Goldsberry, Ray	616-381-3013
Goosefare Promotions	207-284-8657
Greenwald, June	216-932-5535
Grover and Baron	305-754-4931
Gulf Coast Antiques Shows	512-682-6403
Gurley, Nan	207-625-3577
Hannam, Trudy	414-377-5092
Hanson Promotions	319-644-2710
Hanson, Ray	715-842-4112

Hatfield, Jack	803-788-7801
Haughton, Brian and Anna	212-355-6110
Heirloom Promotions	919-368-2420
Hengst, Andrew	315-893-7214
Heritage Productions	804-225-8877
Holt's Antiques Shows	603-434-7398
Hornstein, Merle L.	203-457-0368
The Houston Museum Committee	615-267-7176
Humberstone, J. Jordan	312-227-4464
International Shows Management	417-781-4000
JP Promotions	206-825-5380
Jackson, Arthur	703-765-3469
Jacques, Louise	203-261-0578
Johnson and Moir Antiques Shows	612-478-6500
Johnson, Walt and Nancy	515-265-6940
Jones, N. Pendergast	212-986-8897
Justinius Management	203-259-8706
KJR Joint Venture	904-269-2431
Katona and Lutz	207-338-1444
Kimble, Warren	
King Antiques Shows	904-269-2431
Kline, S.	315-589-8187
Knight, Bruce and Shari	513-325-0053
Koehn, Donald	319-396-3836
Kohls, Paul	513-922-5265
Kramer, Richard E. Management	314-862-1091
Kromer, Ted	216-369-5357
L-W Promotions	317-674-6450
Lake County Promotions	312-223-1433
The Lakeside Group	312-787-6858
Lambeth's Management	803-585-7912
Larsen, Walter and Associates	415-771-3492
Lich, Rod	812-951-3454
Lutz, Bob	207-338-1444
Lyric Management	512-472-5927

M & M Enterprises	313-469-1706
M.I.A. Antiques Show	612-870-3039
MO Productions	513-353-2688
Mackey, Don	603-363-4515
Maddox, Shirley	404-458-1614
Mancuso, David and Peter	215-794-5009
Maron, Bud and Muriel	516-822-2372
Mathieu, J. A. "Jake"	413-245-3436
The Maven Company	203-755-5278
May, Richard	Brimfield, MA 01010
McHugh Presentations	508-384-3857
Michigan Antiques Festival Management	517-793-8389
Mid-America Management	312-530-8558
Midwest Antique Guild	507-368-9343
Miller, Sy Productions	619-436-3844
Milwaukee County Historical Society	414-273-8288
Min & Museum Auxiliary	901 Edgehill Rd., Charlotte, NC 28207
Mongenas	513-321-3885
Montell, James	207-582-2849
Murray, Rebecca	312-446-0537
Needles, Elva	816-747-9619
Nordell Management	313-420-3237
O'Bannon Shows	804-288-5451
O'Brien Enterprises	603-357-2797
The Old Show	412-228-3045
Palko, Edwin T.	
Pitts, Dova	319-242-0139
Promotions	414-723-5651
Reynolds, Jim	614-882-7546
Rogers, Sims	301-228-8858
Rowe, Lillyann H.	207-324-2744
St. George Management	519-448-1140

Salas Concessions	615-383-7635
Savell and Schluter	409-478-6562
Schafer, David	203-245-4173
Schaut, Norman	609-641-4004
Schlecker, Barry	302-571-7407
Schorr, Rosemary and Barry Dobinsky	215-775-5133
Schwartz, Arthur	602-247-1004
Scott Promotions	416-436-1634
Seigert, Gloria	313-421-0762
Shador/Manor House	301-924-2551
Show Promotion	617-229-2414
Sideli, Jacqueline	518-392-6711
Smith, Emily Shows	518-899-2328
Smith, Sanford L. and Associates	212-777-5218
Southwest Antiques Guild	602-282-2213
Southwest MO's	417-883-2449
Stella Show Management Co.	201-368-1130
Stewart, Peggy, Antiques Shows, Inc.	215-388-7601
Stockwell Promotions	614-267-8163
Sturza, Evelyn	301-565-9321
Success Promotions	203-762-7031
Swift, Claudette and Grant	517-263-3115
Titsworth Productions	512-249-3679
Town and Country Antiques Management	703-780-9200
Tri Delta Alumni Show Management	214-369-1509
Turney, Emma Lee	713-520-8057
United Voluntary Services	415-343-3663
Van Deest, Paula	319-365-8446
Van Kuren, Ruth and Dale	716-741-2606
Vintage Promotions	614-486-4991
Wagner Promotions, Inc.	816-539-3305
Walters, Bill, Shows, Inc.	914-758-6186
Welytok, Jim	414-384-4266
Wendy, Diane	914-698-3442

Western Antiques Expositions	206-868-8943
Weston Antiques Show Management	802-824-6645
Wiething Promotions	414-692-2192
Williams, Betty	704-596-4643
Willmann's Shows	312-898-0095
Wirfs, Don and Associates	503-245-6872
Wordell, Richard	401-789-0390
World Wide Antiques Shows Productions	800-525-2729
Wright, Doug, Productions	213-656-5470
Zehule, Vanita	314-742-3400
Zurko's Midwest Promotions	715-526-9769

BIBLIOGRAPHY

The following short list represents the little that has heretofore been written on the mechanics of running an antiques and collectibles business. Most of these texts deal with a single specific area, such as flea markets or auction, but they are included for their in-depth coverage of these topics.

Barlow, Ronald S. *How to Be Successful in the Antique Business*. New York: Charles Scribner's Sons, 1979.

Bursten, Joan, and Louanne Norris. *How to Make Money in the Flea Market: A Practical Guide for Dealers and Customers*. New York: E. P. Dutton, 1978.

DiNoto, Andrea, and Cathy Cashion. *Trash or Treasure*. New York: Crown Publishers, Inc., 1977.

Dorn, Sylvia O'Neill. *The How to Collect Anything Book: Treasure to Trivia with Lots, Little or No Money*. Garden City, N.Y.: Doubleday & Company, Inc., 1976.

Fendlelman, Helaine and Schwartz, Jeri. *Money In Your Attic*. New York: Simon & Schuster, 1985.

Gilbert, Anne. *Investing in the Antiques Market*. New York: Grosset & Dunlap, Inc., 1980.

Jenkins, Emyl. *Why You're Richer Than You Think*. New York: Rawson, Wade Publishers, Inc., 1982.

―――. *Emyl Jenkins Appraisal Book*. New York: Crown Publishers, Inc., 1989.

Ketchum, William C. *Auction: The Guide to Bidding, Buying, Bargaining, Selling, Exhibiting and Making a Profit*. New York: Sterling Publishing Company, Inc., 1980.

Klamkin, Marian and Charles. *Investing in Antiques and Popular Collectibles for Pleasure and Profit*. New York: Funk & Wagnalls, Inc., 1975.

Rush, Richard H. *Antiques as an Investment*. New York: Bonanza Books, 1968.

Sommer, Elyse. *How to Make Money in the Antiques and Collectibles Business: A Complete Career Guide to Starting or Expanding Your Own Business*. Boston: Houghton Mifflin Company, 1979.

Wagenvoord, James. *Cashing in on the Auction Boom*. New York: Rawson, Wade Publishers, Inc., 1980.